Introduction to Takaful

Adnan Malik • Karim Ullah

Introduction to Takaful

Theory and Practice

palgrave
macmillan

Adnan Malik
Centre for Excellence in Islamic Finance
Institute of Management Sciences
Peshawar, Pakistan

Karim Ullah
Centre for Excellence in Islamic Finance
Institute of Management Sciences
Peshawar, Pakistan

ISBN 978-981-32-9015-0 ISBN 978-981-32-9016-7 (eBook)
https://doi.org/10.1007/978-981-32-9016-7

Cover pattern © Melisa Hasan
Cover design: eStudio Calamar

This Palgrave Pivot imprint is published by the registered company Springer Nature Singapore Pte Ltd.
The registered company address is: 152 Beach Road, #21-01/04 Gateway East, Singapore 189721, Singapore

Preface

Globally, insurance and its Islamic alternative called takaful are integral parts of contemporary economic, business and personal activities and provide a risk transform framework for various levels of transactions. Metaphorically, insurance and takaful resemble the financial shock-absorbers that protect entities, including individuals, businesses and even global economies, against risks that are realised, for which the entities do not have any financial plans or any financial capacity to deal with. Unfortunate events that can lead to such situations include death, fire, road accidents, muggings, among many others.

While working in insurance and takaful companies and in the associated education sectors, we have always felt that there is a need to increase awareness of insurance, placing more emphasis on takaful, which is considered to be compliant with the Muslims' beliefs. One way to increase and sustain awareness is to educate students about takaful by including it in academic programmes of study. This could have a long-term impact on this new and developing industry.

Now, many universities around the world, particularly in Asia (e.g., Malaysia, Pakistan), Middle East and in the leading educational centres worldwide, including the UK and the USA, have introduced takaful as subject to the students' management sciences. As a result, we needed to develop new course plans and research reference texts. We realised that there were relatively few relevant books available on the market, and those that did exist were written primarily for practitioners. It would seem to be very difficult for students to learn about the concept of insurance and takaful from these books, especially within the timeframe of a single semester. Therefore, we came up with the idea of authoring a book on takaful for beginner students by documenting our scientific observations and narrative practice of the field. To this end, the content of this book is structured in a logical way that develops students' thinking, starting with simple insurance concepts and moving on to the specialised processes and techniques of takaful. The text includes real and generalisable case studies and templates from our partner in the takaful sector, Pak–Qatar Takaful Company Limited, and some feedback that the authors received.

Chapter 1 explores insurance, one of the techniques for managing risk, in more detail. It focuses on the concept of insurance, its history, its principles and the benefits for individuals and society. In Chap. 2, risk management and the concept of insurance are discussed in the light of Shariah. It explains the objections raised by Islamic scholars to insurance, which are riba (interest), gharar (uncertainty), maysir and qimar (gambling). Chapter 3 introduces the concept of takaful and how it addresses Islamic scholars' objections to insurance. Mini case studies and case studies are provided to clarify the concepts further. Takaful is practised in various countries by adopting models based on partnership contracts, such as mudarabah (a partnership between capital and expertise) and wakalah (where a fee is provided for the service). Chapter 4 of this book discusses the concept of risk and risk-management techniques and how insurance and takaful work as risk-management techniques. Chapter 5 discusses takaful models, placing special emphasis on the most recent model developed. Chapter 6 discusses the different types of takaful cover available, including family (life), health, motor, fire, cash and marine. It sets out how takaful companies acquire, price and deliver these types of cover.

Chapter 7 discusses the concept of takaful, and Chap. 8 discusses the channels for delivering takaful services to participants. These include exclusive agents, independent agents and brokers, the Internet and banca-takaful, among others. Chapter 8 covers the activities related to underwriting in takaful. In underwriting, an applicant's fitness for takaful cover is assessed and a fair contribution (price) for the cover is determined. This involves gathering information about the applicant, evaluating that information and then deciding whether or not to offer takaful to the applicant.

When a defined loss occurs, the litmus test of any takaful company begins. Best practice demands the rejection of fraudulent claims and the swift payment of genuine ones. Chapter 10 focuses on how takaful companies can provide claim services. General takaful claims are usually processed by a surveyor. Therefore, this chapter also explains the surveyor's role in detail, using case studies.

Chapter 11 discusses the role of the regulator in monitoring and supervising takaful companies. Takaful companies claim Shariah compliance; therefore, the regulator should have the monitoring and supervisory systems in place that ensure the observance of Shariah in addition to overseeing the financial aspects of takaful companies.

This book still has room for improvement, so we invite readers to post their feedback and suggestions on the book's Facebook page. Based on new additions, editing and suggestions, we may publish revised versions of this book.

Peshawar, Pakistan — Adnan Malik
Peshawar, Pakistan — Karim Ullah

Acknowledgements

We are very thankful to our students of takaful course and participants of our trainings on takaful, who made us realise to author this book. Their questions and discussions set the path for the narratives in the book, and they proved as research locales for ideas generation, improvements and testing towards this book. Moreover, the completion of this book was not possible without the research support of Centre for Excellence in Islamic Finance, Institute of Management Sciences (CEIF IMSciences) and dedicated team of Pak-Qatar Family Takaful Limited, including Nasir Ali Syed, chief executive officer; Waqas Ahmed, chief operating officer; Syed Fakhre Alam, Kamran Saleem, chief finance officer, Muhammad Saleem, senior manager; Mufti Muhammad Zahid, member Shariah Advisory Board; Mufti Muhammad Akhlaq, Shariah compliance officer; Mufti Muhammad Fawad, Imran Irshad, head of Claims; Muhammad Shahzad, senior manager, head of Underwriting Department, for their significant contributions. We are also grateful to Raza Ali, senior manager, Takaful Pakistan Ltd, for his insightful contributions in the general takaful portion of the book. We are also indebted to our staff CEIF IMSciences, including Shahid Samad Khan, Muhammad Saleem, Muhammad Wahab, Tahira Imtiaz, Obaidullah Khan, Aayat, Laila, Urooj, Reema, Sajida and Muhammad Arif. Special thanks go to Adeel Hamayun for his facilitation. We are specially thankful to our families for supporting us in their time to author this book.

A Note on Research Method for the Book

This book uses a narrative case research methodology, where the data is collected through in-depth participant observations, market research and feedback, and documents as data sources. The concepts, calculations, and discussions are supported through tabulated case studies and exhibits. The book acknowledges the research support of the Centre for Excellence in Islamic Finance, Institute of Management Sciences (CEIF IMSciences), and Pak-Qatar Family and General Takaful Companies, in Pakistan.

Contents

About the Authors

Adnan Malik is serving as a lecturer and industry chair, Centre for Excellence in Islamic Finance, at the Institute of Management Sciences (CEIF IMSciences), Pakistan. He is a certified professional in insurance and takaful, with nearly 15 years of practical experience in reputable insurance and takaful companies. He has also acquired fellowship in life insurance (FLMI) from Life Office Management Association (LOMA) Atlanta, USA, and certification of ACII from Chartered Insurance Institute, UK. He has delivered lectures about takaful on various business and educational forums. He developed multiple courses of takaful in various degree programmes.

Karim Ullah has a PhD on designing Islamic financial services from Brunel University London and executive learning on case method at Harvard Business School. He serves as founding head of the Centre for Excellence in Islamic Finance, Institute of Management Sciences (CEIF IMSciences), Pakistan. He has extensive experience in conducting lectures and trainings on Islamic financial services with regulators and other collaborating Islamic financial institutions around the world. In 2015, Karim led a team of faculty who won the prestigious financial innovation challenge fund, to establish the CEIF, with the support of the State Bank of Pakistan and UK's Department for International Development. Karim has scholarly international books and papers' authorships, and conference presentations on Islamic financial services. He got certifications on training of trainers, training content development, training assessments and training of assessors from Business Edge, IFS, World Bank. He trained academics and bankers on developing and using case studies methods.

List of Figures and Exhibits

List of Tables

CHAPTER 1

Insurance

Abstract This chapter has focused on the concept of insurance to provide a base for the phenomenon of takaful, which is covered in onward chapters. Insurance is a mechanism that enables companies to perform three important functions: to transfer risk, create a common pool and set equitable premiums. These important functions create four main benefits: peace of mind, control of loss, social benefits and economic benefits. Insurance is a well-established business practice, and over time, it has developed its core principles in line with which it operates. These principles include insurable interest, utmost good faith, subrogation, indemnity and proximate cause.

Keywords Insurance • Insurance principles • Premiums • Risk

After reading this chapter, you should understand:

- The concept of insurance
- The history of insurance
- The functions of insurance
- The principles of insurance

A. Malik, K. Ullah, *Introduction to Takaful*,
https://doi.org/10.1007/978-981-32-9016-7_1

Introduction

Takaful is an Islamic alternative to insurance. To better understand how takaful works, it is useful to first explore and understand insurance in terms of how and why it is not considered compliant to the Islamic legal and values system, called Shariah, and how takaful can be an effective alternative. Therefore, this chapter focuses on understanding the basic concept of insurance, its history, its functions and its fundamental principles. Real-life small case studies are provided to aid understanding.

As human beings, we are exposed to several types of risk. In principle, these risks represent deviations from our expectations, which may cause damage to us and our belongings that have value for us. Two such risks are the possibility of losing our life and the possibility of losing our valuable property. In response, people, over a long period of history, have developed techniques to mitigate, transfer and manage these risks, as discussed in Chap. 4. Insurance, if managed properly, can be an effective technique for mitigating and transferring of such physical risks. In a simplest form, an insurance company collects premiums from clients and pays those clients compensation if an insured event occurs. Insurance companies keep these premiums in a fund through which they invest to earn income.

Definition of Insurance

From a clients' point of view, insurance is a mechanism in which a client transfers a financial risk to an entity that provides compensation if an insured event occurs. Different kinds of insurance cover exist to meet clients' different needs; examples include life, health, fire, motor and marine insurance. For such an arrangement of risk cover, there are always at least two parties to an insurance agreement: the insurance company and the client. Cover commences when an agreement is affected between the client and the insurer. The client is also, popularly, called the insured or the policyholder, and such clients can be an individual, company, government or any identifiable entities, such as civil society organisations.

Let us explain the mechanism of a simple insurance with the help of the following two case studies.

Case Study 1.1 Life Insurance
Adam contacts an insurance company to take out a life insurance policy for USD 100,000. If the company agrees to provide this cover, it must pay Adam's nominee a sum of USD 100,000, on the condition if Adam dies. In return, Adam must pay for the cover, USD 5000 a year. Adam agrees and makes his first payment to the insurance company, and the company agrees to provide the cover. Adam is now considered insured by the insurance company.

USD 100,000 is the sum assured, and USD 5000 is the premium. The company will pay a death claim of USD 100,000 to the legal heir if Adam dies, while Adam must pay the company USD 5000 every year. Usually a client will provide the name of their legal heir when they arrange their life insurance. The named legal heir is also called the beneficiary or nominee of the policy. The beneficiary can be the widow, widower, child or/and parent of the client.

Sum assured: USD 100,000
Premium: USD 5000

Case Study 1.2 Car Insurance
Bilal runs a travel company and decides to insure its new fleet of 5 cars worth USD 500,000 and pays a premium of USD 15,000 to the insurance company for a year. Here, USD 500,000 is the sum assured, and USD 15,000 is the premium. The insurance company will cover any costs associated with agreed types of losses the cars experience during the covered period.

Premium: USD 15,000
Sum assured: USD 500,000

A Brief History of Insurance

The development of insurance, as phenomenon, is the result of various problems that humans faced in history, which provide a rationale for why we have such diversified forms of insurance today. In the following, we discuss a brief history of the most common types of insurance policies.

Marine Insurance

Goods have been traded through sea routes for centuries. However, in the past, ships encountered many dangers while at sea and were often destroyed, leaving the merchants destitute and who sometimes die. Chinese merchants, for case study, used to insure the goods that they were transporting through ships to various parts of the world.[1] Upon realisation of defined losses during the voyage, the peer merchants used to join hands and contribute to assist those who had suffered the loss.[2]

In the seventeenth century, it became more common to insure ships and cargoes. For case study, in England, such merchants would meet at coffee houses to agree on insurance contracts. One such coffee house, situated near the River Thames, was owned by Edward Lloyd.[3] Around the year 1688, Edward Lloyd started to encourage merchants to come to his coffee house to carry out their business, because this would bring more business to his coffee house. The merchants attracted insurance experts, who also began frequenting the coffee house in order to get business from the merchants. At that time, the insurance experts would write down the details of the ship and cargo on a piece of paper and sign under a horizontal line.[4] Signing under that line led to the terms underwriter and underwriting being coined, which are still used in insurance. Today, *the underwriter is the expert who decides to accept or reject a client's request for insurance, the sum assured and the premium.*

Today, marine insurance covers all forms of transport: sea, air, rail and road. However, because of its history it is usually called 'marine insurance'.

Fire Insurance

Fire insurance is claimed to have begun after the Great Fire of London in 1666. In that fire, approximately 13,200 homes, 87 churches and dozens of public buildings were destroyed.[5] This unfortunate event compelled

[1] R.L. Carter (Ed.), *Reinsurance*. Springer Science & Business Media, 2013, p. 10.

[2] V. Dover & R.H. Brown, *A handbook to marine insurance: being a textbook of the history, law and practice of an integral part of commerce for the business man and the student*. London: Witherby, 1975, p. XX.

[3] C. Kingston, 'Marine insurance in Britain and America, 1720–1844: a comparative institutional analysis', *The Journal of Economic History*, 67/2(2007), pp. 379–409.

[4] E. Wertheimer, *Underwriting: the poetics of insurance in America, 1722–1872*. Stanford, CA: Stanford University Press, 2006, p. 24.

[5] London Fire Brigade, 'The great fire of London', retrieved 27 October 2016 from www.london-fire.gov.uk/great-fire-of-london.asp.

people to make arrangements for financial compensation when such incidents happened. Insurance companies started establishing themselves during the same period. This marked the beginning of fire insurance. As time passed, one by one, other dangers began to supplement basic fire insurance. These include earthquake, riots and strikes, atmospheric disturbance (flooding, heavy rain, etc.), explosions, aircraft damage and impact damage.

Motor Insurance

Motor insurance was introduced a little later than marine and fire insurance. The first mechanically propelled vehicle appeared on British roads in 1894. At that time the roads were not busy, but there was still a chance of having an accident. Therefore, by 1898, insurance companies had started providing cover to compensate people for losses resulting from accidents involving vehicles.[6] Today, insurance companies mostly provide cover for accidental loss (partial, total and third party) and theft.

Life Insurance

History also shows us that life insurance originated in Italy,[7] where people started to form burial societies, which would collect premiums from participants and pay the burial expenses out of the premiums collected. These societies established pool funds to manage their expenses. Each participant was required to pay an equal amount into the fund. According to Peggy Mace:

> The oldest life insurance policy for which there is surviving evidence was taken out for William Gybbon on 18 June 1583, in London. Gybbon was a salter of fish and meat for the city of London. He bought a one-year policy from Alderman Richard Martin and passed away before the end of the year. At first the company refused to pay, but after some legal wrangling, Martin won the case.[8]

[6] K.J.S. Onge, 'First auto policy sold 110 years ago today', *Insurance Journal*, 27 February 2008, retrieved 27 October 2016 from www.insurancejournal.com/news/national/2008/02/27/87696.htm.

[7] P. Borscheid & N.V. Haueter, *World insurance: the evolution of a global risk network*. Oxford: Oxford University Press, 2012, p. XX.

[8] P. Mace, 'When was the first life insurance policy issued?', *Insurance library*, 28 June 2013, retrieved 18 October 2016 from www.insurancelibrary.com/life-insurance/when-was-the-first-life-insurance-policy-issued.

Functions of Insurance

A contemporary insurance usually performs the following three main functions, as exhibited in Case Study 1.1:

- Providing a risk-transfer mechanism.
- Creating a common pool.
- Setting equitable premiums.

Providing a Risk-Transfer Mechanism

The primary function of insurance is to transfer risk from insured to insurance company, against a premium.

Let us explain the risk-transfer mechanism with the help of Case Study 1.3.

Case Study 1.3 Transferring Risk
Caroline owns a car worth USD 60,000. The car is one of Claire's most valuable possessions. If it is stolen or damaged, Caroline understands that it will cost her a handsome amount of her hard-earned money.

To manage these and other risks associated to her car, Caroline contacts an insurance company to explain these concerns and asks to arrange insurance for the car. The insurance company tells Caroline that they are willing to accept the risk in exchange for a premium of USD 18,000. If Caroline pays the premium, the car will be insured against the risk of theft and accidental damage for 12 months, starting with the date of insurance contract signed by parties.

Caroline agrees and pays the premium to the insurance company; the agreement is put in place and the insurance company issues an insurance policy containing all the details of the contract. The insurance policy will not stop the car being stolen or damaged, but if either of these losses occurred, the insurance company will pay Caroline financial compensation to cover the costs involved.

Therefore, we can say that Caroline has transferred the risk of financial loss to the insurer company in exchange for paying a premium.

Creating a Common Pool

As explained earlier in this chapter, merchants once had to transport their goods by ship. Navigational skills were not as good as they are today, so the merchants were exposed to many dangers.[9] It was quite common for goods to be destroyed, and the merchants had to bear huge financial losses when this happened. To manage this risk, fellow merchants would contribute money to compensate merchants when they suffered a loss.

This arrangement certainly removed the risk of total loss from any one merchant, as each of them knew that their loss would be compensated. However, the problem with this arrangement was that it was not certain that the mutual contribution from the merchants would provide full compensation for the loss. Moreover, because the merchants agreed to share any losses that occurred, they knew how much they had to contribute only after the loss took place. If there was no loss, they would have nothing to pay, but if there were losses, then the exact amount could only be determined after the event.

This raises the question: can we know what the loss will amount to in advance? The answer is yes—we can estimate an expected amount of loss if we create a common pool to which a large number of clients contribute. For case study, if a company wants to provide fire insurance for 10,000 homes, it can look at statistics that show how many homes are damaged by fire in one year. The company can then extrapolate that information to predict how many of the 10,000 homes it wishes to insure will be damaged by fire. It is difficult to predict whether or not a particular house will be damaged by fire, but we can comfortably assess how many homes will be damaged by fire, with some good estimates.

The size of the pool is important here. Let us suppose a homeowner approaches an insurance company to arrange fire insurance. The company tells the homeowner that it is not providing fire insurance at the moment, because fewer than 50 people want it. From looking at the statistics, the company knows that in every 10,000 homes, four are damaged by fire in a single year. Collecting premiums from only 50 clients does not create a large pool, which makes it difficult for the company to offer cover. However, a few months later, a fire breaks out in a house in that area and causes serious damage. Hearing about this event, a large number of clients realise that they need fire insurance and approach the company. Now, if the company provides fire insurance to 10,000 clients, each with a home worth USD 1 million, the company can see that, based on statistics, 4 out of these 10,000 homes may

[9] C.F. Trenerry, *The origin and early history of insurance: including the contract of bottomry.* Lawbook Exchange, 1926.

be damaged. Therefore, the total cost of the claims would be USD 4 million (1 million × 4). To make sure it has enough money in the pool to cover the cost of the expected claims, the company charges an annual premium of USD 400 to every client. The large size of the pool has enabled the company to offer cover that it could not otherwise have provided.

In managing a common pool, the insurer benefits from the law of large numbers. According to this law, *the higher the number of similar situations covered, the more the actual number of events occurring will tend towards the expected number of events.*

Based on this knowledge, the insurer can decide a premium, and the client knows, depending on the type of cover purchased, that they will not have to pay anything more at the end of the year.

Case Study 1.4 Risk Pooling (Life Insurance)

Total number of clients taking out life insurance: 10,000 (A)

Age of all clients: 35 years

Sum assured for each policy: USD 1 million (B)

Number of clients expected to die within a year: 21 (C)

Total amount to be paid in death claims: (B × C) = USD 21 million (D)

Premium to be charged to every client: (D ÷ A) = USD 2100

In this case study, USD 2100 million is the minimum amount of premium that an insurance company should charge for paying death claims only. This is also called the risk premium. The company can and usually do add administrative expenses and profit for calculating a final premium to be charged from the policyholders.

Setting Equitable Premiums

The first life insurance emerged in Italy with the establishment of burial societies.[10] These societies used to collect premiums from their participants for accumulation in a fund. Each participant had to pay an equal

[10] P. Masci, 'The history of insurance: risk, uncertainty and entrepreneurship', *Business and Public Administration Studies*, 6/1(2011), p. 25.

amount into the fund, which was used to pay a specific amount to cover the burial expenses of participants who died. Later, it was noted that older participants of the fund were dying sooner, leaving fewer participants to pay into the fund. The younger participants realised that the society was making a loss, so they began to leave. These types of societies then decided to charge participants individual premiums based on the risk that they each brought to the fund. Today, every client has to pay a premium in accordance with the risk that he or she transfers to the insurance company. *A premium is said to be an equitable premium when it is determined by the specific risk that the individual client is transferring to the insurance company.* This is, perhaps, inspired by the fundamental principles of risk and return,[11] where a return correlates with the level of risk involved in a transaction, an asset or an insurance policy.

The insurer has to make sure that it charges a fair or equitable premium that reflects the risk and value a person or company brings to the pool. This is a complex process to reach to such an equitable premium, and therefore the insurer has to calculate the premium very carefully. In companies offering life and health insurance, actuaries calculate the premiums. An actuary is a person who is trained and experienced in calculating insurance premiums and pension benefits. The expert makes these calculations based on the probability of future incidences, developing creative policies to reduce the probability of undesirable events, and their impacts.[12]

Although the premium charged should be enough to cover the claims made, it should also be competitive, because there are always multiple insurers in the market. If the premium is too high, the insurer will lose business. On the other hand, if the premium is too low, the contributions to the pool have the possibility that they would come to less than the cost of paying claims, which would result in a loss for the company. However, lowering the premiums also increases the possibility of the numbers of contributors to the funds, which can provide the insurer an advantage through the concept of large number. Charging equitable premium ensures sufficient funds in the pool which enable the insurer to take risk of issuing different types of coverage.

[11] W.F. Sharpe, 'Capital asset prices: a theory of market equilibrium under conditions of risk', *The Journal of Finance*, 19/3(1964), pp. 425–442.

[12] Society of Actuaries, 'What do we do?', *Be an actuary*, retrieved 26 October 2016 from www.beanactuary.com/what/do/?fa=what-do-we-do.

The three functions of insurance are thus interdependent, as creating a common pool and calculating equitable premiums all help to provide a sound risk-transfer mechanism.

Benefits of Insurance

A sound insurance market is an essential component of any successful economy, and that is why in many economies, insurance is considered mandatory in many cases. There is also a close link between insurance and industrial development. This section discusses some of the most important benefits of insurance.

Peace of Mind

The knowledge that the financial consequences of certain risks will be met gives peace of mind to those who buy insurance. Peace of mind is important to individuals who insure their car, home or life, but it is also of vital importance to industry and commerce. For case study, why should someone invest in a business venture when there are so many risks that they could lose their money? Yet if people do not invest in business, there will be fewer jobs, fewer goods available and a general reduction in wealth. People feel able to invest in businesses because they transfer some of the biggest risks to an insurer. This gives them the peace of mind they need to do business.

Case Study 1.5 shows how insurance has benefited a business providing a service to society.

Case Study 1.5 Transport Services

Company AL-X provides transport services to people living in the city. An angry mob attacked the company buses parked at the depot, and several buses were burned. AL-X was facing a huge loss, and people expected this to force the company to shut down its operations in the city. However, because the buses were insured, the insurance company paid the claim for the cost of repairing and replacing the damaged buses. As a result, the company's buses are still on the roads, and the people are still enjoying their great service. In this case, we can say that the mechanism of insurance made it possible for AL-X to continue providing the service.

Insurance also acts as a stimulus for business activity. This is done by freeing up funds, so they can be invested in the productive side of a business. Medium and large businesses may create reserves by setting aside funds to cover financial losses caused by fire, theft and other accidents. That money then sits idle until an emergency happens. However, businesses can purchase insurance for a premium that is far lower than the funds they would need to keep in reserves to meet the costs of an emergency. This frees up the firm to do business with the money that they would otherwise have to keep in reserve, resulting in business expansion.

Controlling Loss

Insurance is primarily concerned with the financial consequences of loss, but it would be fair to say that insurers do much more than compensate those who are insured when a loss happens. Insurers have an interest in reducing the frequency and severity of losses by promoting the use of methods to prevent or reduce loss. This function of insurance not only enhances insurers' profitability but also contributes to reducing the general waste that results from losses.

In the eighteenth century, in the UK, insurers used to maintain their own fire brigades, which had fire-fighting equipment. Insurers would make marks on the front doors of the houses that they insured so that it would be easy for their fire brigade to locate the houses covered by the company.[13] For case study, if a whole row of houses was on fire, they might focus on saving the ones that were insured before the ones that weren't. So, some extra incentives are provided for a prioritised cover.

When a person insures their business, such as a factory or a shop, insurers advise them to install fire extinguishers, smoke alarms and sprinkler systems so that a fire can be detected and put out more quickly, and thus losses can be reduced. Insurers offer discounts on the premium if fire-fighting equipment or fire alarms are installed in the building to be insured. Insurers, usually, advise that a tracker (a satellite-based tracking device) be fitted in vehicles to reduce the risks associated with theft. Some insurance companies provide the tracking device, while others give discounts on the premium if the client fits their own tracker in their vehicle.

[13] T. Lambert, 'A brief history of fire fighting', *A world history encyclopedia by Tim Lambert*, retrieved 2 November 2016 from www.localhistories.org/firefighting.html.

Social Benefits

Providing financial compensation to a business if a loss occurs enables the businesses to sustain and continue, as we exhibited in the Case Study 1.5 of AL-X. This ensures that any loss of jobs, goods or services is much smaller than it could have been if no insurance was in place.

Case Study 1.6 shows how this works in practice.

Case Study 1.6 Social Benefits of Insurance

A good-health pharmaceutical manufacturing unit employs 100 people. Fire breaks out in the factory, resulting in major damage to machinery and the factory building. The loss is very large, and the business owner does not have the funds to bear it. The good-health pharma has no money to rebuild the factory; it has to be closed down, resulting in the loss of 100 jobs, and the good medicines will no longer be produced.

However, if the factory building and the machinery had been insured against the risk of fire, there would have been no need for the business to close, because the insurer would have paid the claim to the manufacturer and the factory would have been rebuilt with that money. The business would have continued, avoiding the loss of jobs and medicines.

Economic Benefits

Insurers receive money in the form of premiums from their policyholders. There is always a time gap between when a premium is received and when a claim occurs; for case study, a premium may be received in January and a claim may occur in November. The insurer has all the money from premiums at their disposal, which they can invest.

Insurers invest in a wide range of opportunities. They provide loans to banks and leasing companies, which, in turn, provide financing to the entrepreneurs and businesses that keep the economy running. Such investments are the result of millions and billions of dollars savings in the form of premiums paid to insurers.

Long-term life insurance encourages a good attitude and aptitude to saving money. The long-term life insurance policies are usually for more than five years. If a client survives the whole period of insurance, the insurance company pays a lump sum amount based on the sum assured and the premiums paid by the client. In general insurance, however, no amount is paid to the client if the event covered, such as a car accident or fire, does not happen. So, the concept of personal saving that exists in life insurance is missing in general insurance. Life insurance thus overall enhances inflow of the investments to the economic cycle.

Let us look at another case study to explain how insurance benefits the economy.

Case Study 1.7 Investment Benefits of Insurance
Ayaz decided to take out life insurance cover. As an individual client Ayaz cannot avail all the institutional investment opportunities, because of lack of expertise and legal constraints. However, when Ayaz added the premium to the premiums paid by thousands of other people, a reasonable amount of money is available for institutional investment, which can be managed by experts as pool managers. Thus, the insurance premium that Ayaz added to the billions of dollar premiums from other publicity holders has collectively increased investment in the economy.

Principles of Insurance

The insurance contract between the client and the insurer is based on the principles of:

- Insurable interest
- Utmost good faith
- Subrogation
- Indemnity
- Proximate cause

Insurable Interest

The principle of insurable interest means that there must be a relationship between the client and the beneficiary. Further, the beneficiary must be someone who would suffer if the insured event happened. Typically, insurable interest is established by ownership, possession or any other direct relationship. In life insurance, insurable interest exists due to an established relationship between the client (insured) and the beneficiary. For case study, a wife has an insurable interest in the life of her husband, and vice versa. In such a case, the husband is the client, while the wife is the beneficiary having insurable interest. Many other social relationships set up an insurable interest in life cover. For case study, a client can also name their parents or children as beneficiaries.

In general insurance, the ownership of property usually indicates the insurable interest. The owner of a car or a building can take insurance for that car or building, as the owner has an insurable interest in their own property. So, the client must have an interest in the subject matter of the policy, such as vehicle, building and physical stock. If they don't, the policy is considered void and cannot be enforced by law, because it is regarded as a form of gambling. Usually, an individual must have and demonstrate an insurable interest when they would get some sort of financial benefit from preserving the subject matter or would suffer a financial loss if it were destroyed or damaged, otherwise the situation can create a conflict of interest from the beneficiary point of view, if a beneficiary sees earning in the destruction of property.

Utmost Good Faith

Under the duty of utmost good faith, a client has to convey all the vital (material) information to the insurer before the contract is put in place. Information is material if it may affect the insurer's decision on whether to approve or reject the request for insurance. For case study, in life insurance, a person who works for the police must disclose their profession to the insurer because it can affect the insurer's decision to issue insurance and the cost of the premium. If someone deliberately conceals material information, the insurer has the right to reject the claim.

When a client arranges insurance with a company, on the one hand the client can learn about the insurance company by looking at its website or brochures, can hear from the company agents and so forth. But on the other hand, the insurer company is less likely to have material information about the client—especially those factors that can influence the company's decision on whether to accept the client's request for insurance. Usually, the company finds out about the client by asking questions in an application form. Therefore, there is always a chance that the client may conceal information that may result in their application being rejected or increase the premium. For case study, the client may conceal information about their job or health. The insurer has to make an agreement with the client based on the information the client has provided. So, to avoid the insurer being at a disadvantage, the principle of utmost good faith is added to the insurance contract. This principle gives the insurer the right to reject the client's claim if the client has concealed material information from the insurer.

Indemnity

Through the principle of indemnity, insurance companies claim to return the client, maximally, to the same financial position that they were in before the loss. Companies do this by paying a claim equal to or less than the actual loss to the client, if an insured event occurs. Here, the emphasis is on compensation, which means that a client cannot get any more than the amount that he or she has lost, so that the situation does not lead to any conflict of interest, as if the claim is more than the loss, the beneficiary, would perhaps prefer the insured event to happen.

There is one exception, as in life insurance, if the client dies and the company pays the claim, it still cannot be claimed that the client's family has been returned to the same financial position that they were in before the client's death. Therefore, only contracts of general insurance are contracts of indemnity.

Subrogation

The principle of subrogation empowers an insurer to claim any benefit that may arise from the insured subject matter to which it is entitled to, once it has paid the claim to the client. Subrogation is based on the principle of indemnity. If a company compensates a client in full, the client has no right to seek further compensation, because the principle of indemnity says that a client cannot make a profit if the insured event occurs. Through subrogation, the insurer assumes the rights of the insured, once the indemnity is paid. For case study, if there is an establishment of a responsibility on a third party, other than the insurer and the insured, then the insurer may assume that any benefits receivable from the third party will go to the insurer, if the insured is fully paid with indemnity by the insurance.

Proximate Cause

In insurance, the basic cause that triggers the chain of events resulting in damage is called the proximate cause. For case study, if an earthquake causes short-circuiting in a house and this leads to the house catching fire, the proximate cause is the earthquake, not the short circuit. In such a case, the claim will be considered only if the insurance policy includes cover for earthquakes. In motor insurance, insurance companies cover accidental damage. Thus, if an engine of a car stops working due to its internal fault, that won't be compensated, as the covered proximate cause is accidental loss to the car. In accidental death insurance, the company will pay to the beneficiary if the cause of death is accident. In such a case, finding the main (proximate) cause of death becomes important. The evaluators would need to create cause and effect paths to determine the proximate cause, to decide whether to honour the claim or not, and if that is covered or not.

In this book, we refer to the proximate cause as the event covered.

Chapter Summary

This chapter has focused on the concept of insurance to provide a base for the phenomenon of takaful, which is covered in the following chapters. Insurance is a mechanism that enables companies to perform three important functions: to transfer risk, create a common pool and set equitable premiums. These important functions create four main benefits: peace of mind control of loss, social benefits and economic benefits. Insurance is a well-established business practice, and over time it has developed its core principles in line with which it operates. These principles include insurable interest, utmost good faith, subrogation, indemnity and proximate cause.

CHAPTER 2

Insurance from the Shariah Perspective

Abstract In this chapter, the concept of insurance has been analysed from the perspective of Shariah. Shariah set out Quranic verses and Ahadith that support risk management. Insurance has elements of riba, maysir and gharar, which make it non-permissible from the Shariah perspective. There are two types of riba: riba al Quran and riba al Hadith. Riba al Quran is a conditional or understood increase versus a loan or debt, while riba al Hadith is excess compensation without any consideration resulting from the sale of specific goods. Both types of riba are present in insurance. Gharar has an Arabic root meaning 'absence' or 'insufficient information', which causes uncertainty. This may exist in a contract, price, subject or transaction outcome. There are degrees of gharar, and excessive gharar is prohibited. Excessive gharar leads to undue loss for one party and unjustified gain for the other, which is prohibited. Maysir also exists in insurance. In maysir, the parties involved put the ownership of their property in danger by linking it with the occurrence of an uncertain event. The outcome is always one party's gain at the expense of the other.

Keywords Gharar • Maysir • Riba

A. Malik, K. Ullah, *Introduction to Takaful*,
https://doi.org/10.1007/978-981-32-9016-7_2

After reading this chapter, you should understand:

- The concept of insurance from the Shariah perspective
- The concepts of protection, investment and expenses in insurance
- The generic insurance model
- The elements of insurance that are not permissible from the Shariah perspective

Introduction

From the discussion in Chap. 1, we can conclude that insurance is essentially a risk-transfer mechanism, where the insured entity transfers its risk to the insurer entity—on a price called premium, if that is commercial insurance. From the insured client's perspective, insurance could be interpreted as a risk-mitigation tool because with it we transfer risk to an insurance company and feel less burdened with the financial loss that may be caused by an accident, a theft, a fire or the death of the head of the household. Takaful, as an alternative to insurance, emerged due to objectives of Islamic scholars on the conventional insurance models and the interpretations of risks that it aims to transfer and mitigate. Shariah, which is the Islamic law, provides an alternative faith and rationality based on the premises for establishing this new model of transferring and mitigating risks associated with life and valuables.

Risk Mitigation from the Shariah Perspective

Shariah provides a comprehensive set of norms and rulings based upon the verses from the holy Quran and sayings and doings of the Prophet Muhammad, peace be upon him. According to the Shariah rulings, risk mitigation as a function is not only permissible but also encouraged. God Almighty narrates the story of the Prophet Yousuf, يوسف عليه السلام, in relation to financial planning:

قَالَ اجْعَلْنِي عَلَىٰ خَزَآئِنِ الْأَرْضِ إِنِّي حَفِيظٌ عَلِيمٌ ﴿٥٥﴾

He said: 'Appoint me to (supervise) the treasures of the land. I am indeed a knowledgeable keeper.' (Surah Yusaf: 55)

It is also mentioned in a Hadith:

> 'O Messenger of Allah! Shall I tie it [the camel] and rely [upon Allah], or leave it loose and rely [upon Allah]?' He said: 'Tie it and rely [upon Allah].'

Islam, therefore, encourages the followers to take measures to reduce risk, provided that the procedures and mechanisms are within the Shariah rulings. Shariah objects to the way in which risk is mitigated through insurance because of the presence of riba (interest), gharar (uncertainty) and maysir or qimar (gambling), which are discussed later on in this chapter. Therefore, any risk-mitigation system that does not contain these prohibited elements can be acceptable from the Shariah point of view.

COOPERATION

Shariah encourages cooperation and brotherhood. As mentioned in the definition of insurance, the loss of one is paid for by many, which promotes cooperation among people. An insurance company collects a small amount of money in the form of a premium from many clients, and when losses to a few of those clients occur, they are compensated using the money collected from the many. Such compensation is made possible through clients' cooperation with each other. Islam supports cooperation in society when it is for a good cause and does not lead to any unjust processes and consequences.

In the Holy Quran, Allah talks about helping each other for good causes:

وَتَعَاوَنُوا۟ عَلَى ٱلْبِرِّ وَٱلتَّقْوَىٰ ۖ وَلَا تَعَاوَنُوا۟ عَلَى ٱلْإِثْمِ وَٱلْعُدْوَٰنِ ۚ ﴿٢﴾

> Help each other in righteousness and piety and do not help each other in sin and aggression.

إِنَّمَا ٱلْمُؤْمِنُونَ إِخْوَةٌ ﴿١٠﴾

> All believers are but brothers.

The Mechanism of Insurance

From the earlier discussion, it is evident that Islam supports and encourages risk mitigation if the mechanism for doing so does not contain any non-permissible elements. The mechanism of insurance contains riba, gharar and qimar which make it non-permissible in Islam. Insurance and takaful are both risk-mitigation tools, but there are differences in how they work. The mechanism of takaful is permissible, while the mechanism of insurance is not permissible.

How the Insurance System Works

In insurance, customers buy protection against the risk of financial loss caused by certain events, such as death, accident, burglary and damage to property from fire or flooding. At the same time, life insurance provides the additional benefits of saving and investment, as it encourages clients to get into the habit of saving part of their income. The attributes of protection, investment and expenses are at the core of how the insurance system operates. These are discussed in more detail in the following section.

Protection, Investment and Expenses in Insurance

Based on the services available, insurance can be grouped into two categories: life insurance and non-life (or general) insurance. In life insurance, the company divides the received premium into three portions: protection, investment and expenses. In general insurance, the company divides the received premium into two portions: protection and expenses. There is no element of savings in general insurance—the division between protection and expenses is made only to manage funds.

Protection

Uncertainty about future events creates worry and anxiety. These uncertainties may include the risks mentioned previously, which can result in cash outflows. For case study, the death of the only person in a family who is earning an income may result in extreme hardship for the rest of the family. In addition to bereavement, the family has to deal with financial stress. In such a situation, an insurance company can provide effective help. If the person who has died is covered by an insurance company, the company may provide handsome financial compensation to their family, relieving them from the financial stress, at least for a while.

Investment
In life insurance, in addition to the element of risk cover, there is a provision for saving and investment, which results in a return for clients. The premium paid is used to pay claims; and if death does not occur and the period of cover ends (matures), the client is paid a certain amount (a maturity claim) depending on the agreement.

Let us explain it with the help of a case study.

Case Study 2.1 Maturity Claim
Person A buys the following life insurance policy:
Sum assured: USD 100,000
Duration of cover: 20 years
Annual premium: USD 3000

After paying the annual premium of USD 3000 for 20 years, the policy ends, and Person A is still alive. Therefore, no claim was made under the policy and Person A is paid the following amount:
Sum assured: USD 100,000
Profit: USD 400,000
Amount paid to Person A: USD 500,000.

Expenses
While providing services to clients, an insurance company incurs the following expenses.

- The cost of paying claims to clients when insured events happen.
- Administration costs, which may include salaries, rent and taxes.
- Dividends for shareholders (although this is not strictly an expense, it is an outflow for the company as entity).

The Generic Insurance Model

In this section, we explain the mechanism of insurance as a generic model with the help of Case Study 2.2 and Fig. 2.1.

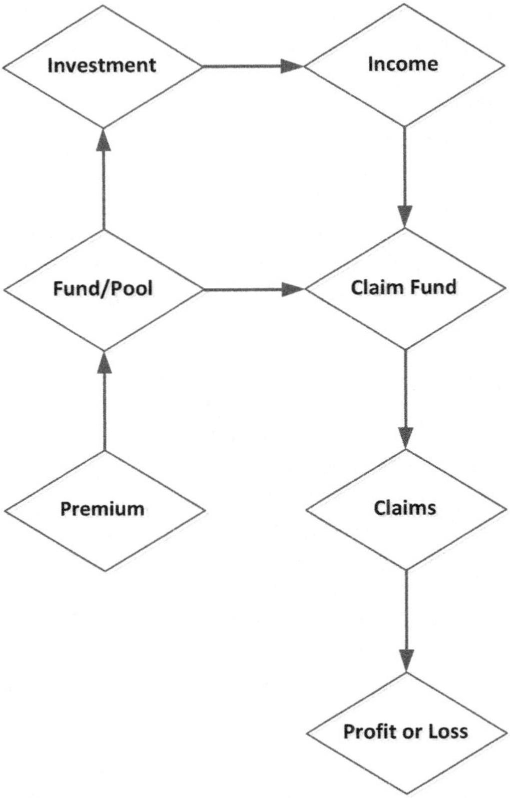

Fig. 2.1 A simplified model of insurance

In this model, insurance companies offer policies (such as life, motor and health insurance) to clients in exchange for a premium. Clients buy policies that meet their needs by paying premiums to insurance companies. Each insurance company places all the premiums they receive into a pool fund, which is then invested in safe, income-generating businesses. Usually, there is a time gap between the payment of a premium and the occurrence of an insured event. So, to benefit from this, insurers invest the pool fund in various ways in order to earn income that can be used to pay clients' claims.

Income from investments plays an important role in the overall profitability of an insurance company. Together, the pool money and investment income make up the claim fund. If the company's total expenses, including the cost of paying claims, come to less than the amount held in the claim fund, the company is said to be in profit; if the opposite is true, the company is said to have suffered a loss. If the collected premiums come to less than the cost of the claims, the company bears an underwriting loss. The company can be in profit despite having an underwriting loss if the income from investment is greater than the underwriting loss.

Let's explain this with the help of a case study.

Case Study 2.2 Calculating Profit

Total premiums collected by the company:	USD 100 million (A)
Income earned on investments:	USD 10 million (B)
Total claim amount paid:	USD 70 million (C)
Underwriting profit:	(A – C) =USD 100 million – USD 70 million =USD 30 million (D) Overall profit: (D + B) =USD 30 million + USD 10 million =USD 40 million

The insurance company owns the pool fund. Therefore, the client is not in a position to ask questions about the investments as long as the company honours the claims it has agreed to pay.

Figure 2.1 illustrates a simplified model of conventional insurance. However, in practice, operations are far more detailed and sometimes complex.

Riba, Gharar and Maysir

Insurance is a sale and purchase contract. In Islam, it is not permissible because of the presence of three prohibited elements. So far in this book, we have discussed several benefits that insurance can bring to an economy, institutions and individuals. However, because of the inherent elements of *riba, gharar and qimar* in insurance transactions, Shariah does not permit the operation of insurance, at least in its current form. Therefore, Islamic scholars have declared conventional insurance non-permissible.

Riba

Literally, the word *riba means an excess, increase or addition. In practice, it is the payment and receipt of interest over a principal amount.*[1]

Why Riba Is Prohibited

The Holy Quran prohibits riba in Surah ul-Baqarah, verses 275–281, as follows.

الَّذِينَ يَأْكُلُونَ الرِّبٰوا لَا يَقُومُونَ إِلَّا كَمَا يَقُومُ الَّذِي يَتَخَبَّطُهُ الشَّيْطٰنُ مِنَ الْمَسِّ ۚ ذٰلِكَ
بِأَنَّهُمْ قَالُوٓا إِنَّمَا الْبَيْعُ مِثْلُ الرِّبٰوا ۗ وَأَحَلَّ اللّٰهُ الْبَيْعَ وَحَرَّمَ الرِّبٰوا ۚ فَمَن جَآءَهُۥ مَوْعِظَةٌ مِّن
رَّبِّهِۦ فَانتَهٰى فَلَهُۥ مَا سَلَفَ وَأَمْرُهُۥٓ إِلَى اللّٰهِ ۖ وَمَنْ عَادَ فَأُولٰٓئِكَ أَصْحٰبُ النَّارِ ۖ هُمْ فِيهَا خٰلِدُونَ

Those who benefit from interest shall be raised like those who have been driven to madness by the touch of the Devil; this is because they say: 'Trade is like interest' while God has permitted trade and forbidden interest. Hence those who have received the admonition from their Lord and desist may keep their previous gains, their case being entrusted to God; but those who revert shall be the inhabitants of the fire and abide therein forever. (275)

يَمْحَقُ اللّٰهُ الرِّبٰوا وَيُرْبِي الصَّدَقٰتِ ۗ وَاللّٰهُ لَا يُحِبُّ كُلَّ كَفَّارٍ أَثِيمٍ ﴿٢٧٦﴾

God deprives interest of all blessing but blesses charity; He loves not the ungrateful sinner. (276)

إِنَّ الَّذِينَ ءَامَنُوا وَعَمِلُوا الصّٰلِحٰتِ وَأَقَامُوا الصَّلٰوةَ وَءَاتَوُا الزَّكٰوةَ لَهُمْ أَجْرُهُمْ عِندَ رَبِّهِمْ
وَلَا خَوْفٌ عَلَيْهِمْ وَلَا هُمْ يَحْزَنُونَ ﴿٢٧٧﴾

Those who believe, perform good deeds, establish prayer and pay the zakat, their reward is with their Lord; neither should they have any fear, nor shall they grieve. (277)

[1] M.I.A. Usmani, *Meezan Bank's guide to Islamic banking*. Karachi: Darul-Ishaat, 2015, p. XX.

يَٰٓأَيُّهَا ٱلَّذِينَ ءَامَنُواْ ٱتَّقُواْ ٱللَّهَ وَذَرُواْ مَا بَقِيَ مِنَ ٱلرِّبَوٰٓاْ إِن كُنتُم مُّؤۡمِنِينَ ٢٧٨

O, believers, fear Allah, and give up what is still due to you from the interest [usury], if you are true believers. (278)

فَإِن لَّمۡ تَفۡعَلُواْ فَأۡذَنُواْ بِحَرۡبٖ مِّنَ ٱللَّهِ وَرَسُولِهِۦۖ وَإِن تُبۡتُمۡ فَلَكُمۡ رُءُوسُ أَمۡوَٰلِكُمۡ لَا
تَظۡلِمُونَ وَلَا تُظۡلَمُونَ ٢٧٩

If you do not do so, then take notice of war from Allah and His Messenger. But, if you repent, you can have your principal. Neither should you commit injustice nor should you be subjected to it. (279)

وَإِن كَانَ ذُو عُسۡرَةٖ فَنَظِرَةٌ إِلَىٰ مَيۡسَرَةٖۚ وَأَن تَصَدَّقُواْ خَيۡرٞ لَّكُمۡ إِن كُنتُمۡ تَعۡلَمُونَ ٢٨٠

If the debtor is in difficulty, let him have respite until it is easier, but if you forego out of charity, it is better for you if you realise. (280)

وَٱتَّقُواْ يَوۡمٗا تُرۡجَعُونَ فِيهِ إِلَى ٱللَّهِۖ ثُمَّ تُوَفَّىٰ كُلُّ نَفۡسٖ مَّا كَسَبَتۡ وَهُمۡ لَا يُظۡلَمُونَ ٢٨١

And fear the Day when you shall be returned to the Lord and every soul shall be paid in full what it has earned and no one shall be wronged. (281)

Riba is also prohibited in the Hadith as follows.

- From Jabir r.z

The Prophet (PBUH) may curse the receiver and the payer of interest, the one who records it and the two witnesses to the transaction, and said: 'They are all alike [in guilt].' (Muslim, Kitab al-Musaqat, Bab la'ni akili al-Riba wa mu'kilihi; also in Tirmidhi and Musnad Ahmad)

- From Abu Hurayrah r.z

The Prophet (PBUH), said: 'There will certainly come a time for mankind when everyone will take riba and if he does not do so, its dust will reach him.' (Abu Dawud, Kitab al-Buyu', Bab fi ijtinabi al-shubuhat; also in Ibn Majah)

- From Abu Hurayrah r.z

> The Prophet (PBUH), said: 'God would be justified in not allowing four persons to enter paradise or to taste its blessings: he who drinks habitually, he who takes riba, he who usurps an orphan's property without right, and he who is undutiful to his parents.' (Mustadrak al-Hakim, Kitab al-Buyu')

Types of Riba
There are two types of riba:

- Riba al Quran
- Riba al Hadith

Riba al Quran
Riba al Quran is so called because several verses of the Holy Quran have declared it impermissible. It is defined as a conditional or understood increase versus a loan or debt.[2] It is also called riba an nasiyah.

Verse 39 of the Quran mentions riba al Quran Surah ul-Rum as follows:

> That which you give as interest to increase the people's wealth increases not with God; but that which you give in charity, seeking the goodwill of God, multiplies manifold. (30: 39)

Riba al Quran exists in the investment element of insurance. As mentioned previously, a claim does not usually occur on the first day the premium is paid by the client. There is always a time gap between receiving the premium and paying the claim (if an insured event occurs). To benefit from this time gap, insurance companies invest the premiums in opportunities that bring the safest and best returns. These investments may or may not be Shariah-compliant. A large portion of these investments is made up of interest-bearing loans provided to banks, leasing companies and so on, because these provide a safer and better return. The income earned on these loans is riba al Quran; hence, it is prohibited. Therefore, when claims occur, the money that the insurance company pays to its claimants includes income earned from such investments, which renders the transaction a prohibited one.

Let's look at a case study of how this works in practice.

[2] M.I.A. Usmani, *Meezan Bank's guide to Islamic banking*, pp. 43–44.

Case Study 2.3 Riba al Quran

An insurance company has received USD 10 million in the form of premiums. Instead of leaving the premium payment idle until it is needed to pay a claim, the company invests it for a return. The insurance company needs a safe, good return on investments. This may be provided by non-permissible investments, such as offering interest-bearing loans to banks and leasing companies or investing in the stocks of companies doing business that is not Shariah-compliant. By lending USD 7 million to banks and leasing companies in the form of interest-bearing loans, the insurance company earns a return of USD 1 million. This return is riba al Quran. The company places this amount into the claim fund and uses it to pay clients when they claim for their insured losses.

Riba al Hadith

Riba al Hadith means 'that excess which is taken in exchange of specific homogenous commodities and encountered in their hand-to-hand purchase and sale as explained in the famous hadith'.[3]

In the Dark Ages, only riba al Quran was considered to be riba. However, the Holy Prophet (PBUH) also classified the second form, riba al Hadith, as riba. This is also called riba al fadl.

- From 'Ubada ibn ul-Samit r.z.

The Prophet (PBUH), said: 'Gold for gold, silver for silver, wheat for wheat, barley for barley, dates for dates and salt for salt—like for like, equal for equal and hand-to-hand; if the commodities differ, then you may sell as you wish, provided that the exchange is hand-to-hand.' (Muslim, Kitab al-Musaqat, Bab al-sarfi wa bay'i al-dhahabi bi al-waraqi naqdan; also in *Tirmidhi*)

- From Abu Sa'id r.z

Bilal r.z brought to the Prophet (PBUH), some *barni* [good quality] dates, whereupon the Prophet (PBUH) asked him where these were from. Bilal replied, 'I had some inferior dates which I exchanged (with better quality

[3] M.I.A. Usmani, *Meezan Bank's guide to Islamic banking*, pp. 46–47.

dates) for these—two *sa's* for a *sa'*.' The Prophet said, 'Oh no, this is exactly riba. Do not do so, but when you wish to buy, sell the inferior dates against something [cash] and then buy the better dates with the price you receive.' (Muslim, Kitab al-Musaqat, Bab al-ta'ami mithlan bi mithlin; also *Musnad* Ahmad)

Riba al Hadith also exists in contracts of insurance. When an insurance company pays a claim to the claimant, the claim amount is always higher than the premium paid by the client. Therefore, the excess amount is considered to be riba al Hadith and is prohibited. In this sense, currency is considered as a commodity, and exchanging it is acceptable only if the exchange amounts are equal.

Let's look at a case study of how this works in practice.

Case Study 2.4 Riba al Hadith
Person A buys the following car insurance:

Value of the car: USD 1 million
Annual premium: USD 30,000

The car meets with an accident and the loss is assessed as amounting to USD 40,000. The insurance company pays Person A compensation for the loss. In this case, the client paid USD 30,000 but received USD 40,000 in return. Therefore, the excess of USD 10,000 that the client received is riba al Hadith.

Gharar

Gharar has an Arabic root meaning 'absence' or 'insufficient information', which causes uncertainty. This may exist in a contract, price, subject or transaction outcome. There are degrees of gharar, and excessive gharar is prohibited in Shariah. This is because excessive gharar leads to undue loss for one party and unjustified gain for the other. This causes speculative risk, which leads to undue loss for one party and unjustified enrichment for the other.[4]

[4] H. Ahmed, *Product development in Islamic banks*. Edinburgh: Edinburgh University Press, 2011.

Gharar is said to be present in any agreement in which the duty of one party is clearly set out, while the duty of the other party is not clear. Many classic case studies of gharar are provided explicitly in the Hadith. They include the sale of fish that are still in the sea, birds that are still in the sky and unripe fruits still on the tree, among other case studies. Islam does not allow the presence of excessive uncertainty in sale and purchase transactions, because this may lead to disputes. Remember, insurance is a sale and purchase agreement too.

Gharar in Insurance

Suppose a person buys insurance cover for a car worth USD 600,000 and pays a premium of USD 20,000 to the insurance company. Neither the person nor the insurance company knows whether a loss will occur or, if it does, when the loss will happen and how much it will amount to. If a loss does not occur, the client will lose their money and the insurer will make a profit. If the car is stolen, the client will receive compensation of USD 600,000 and will be in profit (as the client gets USD 580,000 more than they paid), while the insurer will suffer a loss. Therefore, at the time of the agreement it is clear that the client has a duty to pay the premium of USD 20,000 to the company, but the duty of the insurance company is uncertain.

Conditions for Gharar

The conditions required for gharar are as follows.

- There is uncertainty in the commutative agreement (aqd mua'wadat), in which each of the contracting parties gives and receives an equivalent. Sale and purchase is one such agreement.
- There is a lot of uncertainty (gharar e kaseer).
- The uncertainty relates to the main elements of the contract.

Gharar in the Foundations of Insurance

Insurance is a sale and purchase agreement in which the client (the buyer) buys a sum assured from the insurance company (the seller) for a premium. Neither party knows whether a loss will occur or, if it does, what the extent will be. The mechanism of insurance is based on uncertainty: if a person knew that no loss would happen to their property, then they would not need to buy insurance. In the same way, if an insurance company knew that a particular item of property was going to be affected by a loss, it would never sell cover to the owner of that item of property. Hence, this proves that uncertainty exists in abundance in insurance. Because insurance is a sale and purchase agreement, the presence of such excessive uncertainty makes it non-permissible.

Gharar affects the validity of a contract if it is found in the following areas.

- Subject matter: gharar in the type, features or quantity of the object.
- Period: gharar due to the delivery time.
- Price: gharar due to the price or the method of payment.
- Delivery: gharar in relation to the ability to deliver.

Gharar is tolerable if it:

- Is trivial (gharar e yaseer).
- Occurs in contracts other than sale and purchase contracts, such as gratuitous contracts (i.e., making a gift).
- Exists in the ancillary object or appendages only and not in the main subject matter of the contract.

Maysir

The word *maysir*, mentioned in the Holy Quran, is derived from the word *yusr*, which means 'ease'. This meaning indicates that money or goods are acquired or lost easily in gambling and in similar transactions. Technically, maysir is a contract in which profit of one party is loss of the other party based on an uncertain event. Making a profit at the expense of another party's loss without giving that party any product or service in return may also be referred to as maysir.

Conditions for Maysir

For something to be classed as maysir, the following elements are required.

- There is a contract of exchange (mu'awadat) between the parties.
- Under the contract, each party puts its ownership in danger.
- No party has control over the event.
- Each party either loses its property or gains ownership of another party's property.

Let's look at two cases of maysir.

Case Study 2.5 Maysir

Situation A

In Athletics, the 1500 m race is in progress and two spectators decide to make a bet. The first spectator says to the second spectator, 'If A wins, you'll have to give me USD 100, but if B wins, I'll have to give you USD 100.'

Situation B

Two friends are talking about the weather. The first friend says, 'If it rains today, you'll have to give me USD 100, but if it doesn't rain, I'll give you USD 100.'

In each of these cases, neither person has any control over the outcome (who will win the race or whether it will rain), but they are still making a bet. In such a situation, earning money is prohibited because it brings no benefit to society.

Maysir in Insurance

Gambling-like transactions also exist in conventional insurance practice. Let's suppose a client buys one year of home insurance with USD 100,000 of cover and pays an annual premium of USD 2000 to the insurance company. If the client's house is damaged (for case study, by fire) within that year, the company will compensate the client up to USD 100,000, depending on the extent of the damage. If a fire breaks out and the house is burned down, the company will pay USD 100,000. However, if there is no fire, the client will lose their USD 2000. Whether or not a fire breaks out is not within the control of the company or the client. If it happens, the client will receive a net benefit of USD 98,000, and the insurance company will lose that amount; if it does not happen, the client loses USD 2000, and the insurance company will gain that amount.

Insurance companies are commercial organisations that exist for profit. They make a profit when fewer claims occur. The premiums of the clients who do not claim contribute to the profit made by the insurance companies. We can also say that the difference between the total amount received in premiums and the total amount paid in claims adds to the profits made by the insurance company.

Chapter Summary

In this chapter, the concept of insurance has been analysed from the perspective of Shariah. It has set out Quranic verses and Hadith that support risk management. Insurance has elements of riba, maysir and gharar, which makes it non-permissible from the Shariah perspective.

There are two types of riba: riba al Quran and riba al Hadith. Riba al Quran is a conditional or understood increase versus a loan or debt, while riba al Hadith is excess compensation without any consideration resulting from the sale of specific goods. Both types of riba are present in insurance.

Gharar has an Arabic root meaning 'absence' or 'insufficient information', which causes uncertainty. This may exist in a contract, price, subject or transaction outcome. There are degrees of gharar, and excessive gharar is prohibited. Excessive gharar leads to undue loss for one party and unjustified gain for the other, which is prohibited. Maysir (gambling) also exists in insurance. In maysir, the parties involved put the ownership of their property in danger by linking it with the occurrence of an uncertain event. The outcome is always one party's gain at the expense of the other.

CHAPTER 3

Takaful and Its Shariah Compliance

Abstract This chapter has focused on the concept of takaful. Takaful practices existed in the Arab world before the era of Islam, and they were not objected in Islam. The recent practice of takaful emerged in 1979, and there are now more than 300 takaful operators across the globe. Takaful is a contract of tabarru, while conventional insurance is a sale and purchase transaction. The objections to riba al Hadith, maysir and gharar are valid when a contract is commutative, as it is in conventional insurance. However, they are invalid when a contract is non-commutative and is based on tabarru. Therefore, the objections of riba al Hadith, gharar and maysir do not exist in relation to takaful.

Keywords Gharar • Maysir • Riba • Takaful • Tabarru

After reading this chapter, you should understand:

- The history of takaful
- The generic takaful model
- The manner in which objections to insurance are addressed by takaful

A. Malik, K. Ullah, *Introduction to Takaful*,
https://doi.org/10.1007/978-981-32-9016-7_3

Introduction

We take care of our health by eating good-quality food, doing exercise and avoiding things that could damage our health. We keep our doors locked when we are not at home, and we drive carefully to avoid accidents. We take all these precautionary measures to avoid losses, but there is still a chance that something could go wrong. We can become ill, have a car accident or be burgled. All these events bring with them a financial loss, which affects our peace of mind. An individual can go bankrupt if the losses are significant and beyond their assets. This makes it a burden to cover these losses as an individual. However, if we agree to help each other in such events, we can effectively reduce the financial impact of such risks on individual people. The practice of helping each other in times of need is the essence of takaful.

Definition of Takaful

The word *takaful* is derived from the Arabic root word *kafala*, which means guarantee. Takaful means mutual protection and joint guarantee. In practice, takaful refers to participants making mutual contributions to a common fund with the purpose of providing mutual indemnity if certain events occur.

Takaful is a Shariah-compliant arrangement whereby individuals in the community jointly guarantee to protect themselves against future loss or damage. The key parties involved in any takaful arrangement are:

- The participants
- The takaful fund
- The takaful operator (the company or professional managing the fund)

Based on the legal relationships of these parties, takaful can be offered through various models. One of such model is Principal—Agent model with waqf. This model is also called wakalah waqf model. We will read more about takaful models in the coming chapters.

In wakalah waqf model, the takaful fund is managed by the takaful operator, which is an operator only and carries out its role in the form of a wakeel (agent). Unlike an insurance company, a takaful operator doesn't own the takaful fund; it only manages the fund in return for a service fee. Participants make contributions (which are given in the form of donations) to the takaful from which they may benefit if they suffer a loss. All claims are paid by the takaful and not by the takaful operator.

You may be thinking that takaful is just the same as insurance, but it is not. Insurance and takaful are both tools for risk mitigation and financial protection. They serve a similar purpose, but they are not the same in structure. A good analogy to illustrate this is the difference between frozen yoghurt and ice cream. Frozen yoghurt looks and tastes just like ice cream, but it is not ice cream. In general, it serves as an alternative to ice cream—one that is usually lower in fat and calories. It costs about the same, perhaps a little more or less. What is most important, however, is that although frozen yoghurt is a perfect alternative to ice cream, it is one that is healthier. Another analogy is the difference between eating meat from a goat that has been slaughtered in a permissible (halal) way and eating meat from a goat that has not been slaughtered in a permissible way. The differences between the tools available for risk mitigation and financial protection are things that everybody needs to be concerned about. For the tool to be fully effective, it needs to be not only good at mitigating risk but also properly serviced, competitively priced and, importantly, in compliance with the religious beliefs and good for the individual and the community, and takaful seems to be serving both purposes.

History of Takaful

In the pre-Islamic period, various kinds of insurance existed in the Arab world. In the first constitution of Medina in 622 AD, there were codified references to social insurance relying upon practices such as al-diyah and al-aqila (which referred to blood money paid to free someone who stood accused of an accidental killing), fidyah (a ransom for prisoners of war) and cooperative schemes to aid those who were in need, ill or poor.

The first contemporary takaful company was established in Sudan in 1979.[1] In the same year, another takaful company was established in Bahrain. In the 1980s, several takaful companies were established in the Middle East and Malaysia. In Malaysia, the Takaful Act was passed by parliament in 1984.[2] Today, more than 300 takaful companies are operating around the world.

[1] W.J. Kwon, 'Islamic principle and takaful insurance: re-evaluation', *Journal of Insurance Regulation*, 26/1(2007), p. 53.

[2] Takaful Act 1984, Laws of Malaysia Act 312, retrieved 27 October 2016 from www.bnm.gov.my/documents/act/en_takaful_act.pdf.

We have explained that insurance benefits society in many ways. If a system is beneficial, why are there objections to it? The answer is that Islamic scholars do not object to the purpose of insurance, but to the way in which it is practised. Consider milk as a case study: we are permitted to drink milk unless a prohibited drink is added to it. Similarly, insurance also contains prohibited elements, and if they are removed or replaced with permitted elements or processes, the scholars will no longer object.

As discussed earlier, insurance is a risk-transfer mechanism in which the financial risk of a loss is transferred to an insurer. Islamic scholars object to the mechanism of insurance because of the presence of riba, gharar and maysir. Instead, they suggest using the takaful system for risk mitigation.

Takaful is an arrangement between participants of a community in which each participant mutually agrees to help the others in times of need. For case study, a family could be in trouble if they lost the breadwinner's income because of their death, a severe illness or an accident. Imagine the financial distress they would be going through. Isn't it our moral duty to help such families? Takaful is one way of fulfilling this responsibility.

Remember, in future, it could be you or I who need the same help. Therefore, it is important that we help those in distress while we can, safe in the knowledge that others will do the same for us. This is the basic foundation of takaful.

A takaful company establishes a fund and invites people to become participants by contributing a small amount to the fund in return for cover of their needs. Like insurance, the cover can include financial protection for events such as a car accident or theft, or a death benefit if the participant dies. Family takaful protects a person from life-related financial losses, while general takaful deals with other financial losses, such as theft, fire or mishaps at home. Each participant contributes to the fund with the intention that if any participant suffers a loss defined by the fund (for case study, the death of the participant, an accidental damage to a vehicle or a fire in a factory), that participant will be compensated by the fund. How much each participant contributes depends upon the type of cover that they want from the fund and how much risk they bring to the fund.

So, when you decide to become a participant, you regularly donate a small amount, called the contribution, to the takaful fund from your savings as tabarru (donations). If millions of people contributed to the takaful, imagine how much money there would be!

Traditionally, Takaful is similar to a fund established by a big family to help each other financially when someone among them dies. In a family takaful fund, the family may decide that every married man will contribute a specific amount to a takaful fund, which will provide financial assistance to their immediate family members if they die. Similar to a family takaful system, the takaful is a social welfare service. Whenever a participant's family is in financial trouble, the takaful comes to the rescue by compensating them for their loss. In this way, it helps them to overcome their immediate challenges and move on with their lives. However, do not forget, it is the participants of a takaful who make all this happen.

Obviously, as more and more people join, the takaful fund gets larger and larger, we need professionals or a company to look after it. On behalf of the takaful fund, these professionals or companies collect contributions and pay claims from the fund when an event covered occurs (for case study, if a participant dies). Claims are paid only for the losses that the participants have contributed to in their donations to the fund (the respective takaful cover). We need to trust these professionals and companies to make the best decisions for the continuity and sustainability of the takaful system. As mentioned previously, in takaful, the company providing its services and operating the takaful is called the takaful operator or simply the operator.

The contributions received by the takaful operator are further invested in halal (permissible) avenues, as there is always a time gap between receiving contributions and paying claims. The operator, therefore, prudently invests in halal businesses with the aim of increasing the value of the takaful fund and giving returns to participants in exchange for their contributions. A family takaful operator usually establishes two funds: one for risk protection and the other for investment. This system works best if participants contribute regularly and continue their membership for the full term. On top of this, each year the participants share the surplus in the takaful fund. In general takaful, the surplus is the amount left in the takaful fund after paying all the expenses and claims.

Takaful is based on the principles of brotherhood, cooperation, mutuality and solidarity. Although insurance companies claim that they provide a similar service, this is not so. The difference between takaful and insurance is the nature of the contract. An insurance contract contains the prohibited elements of riba, gharar and maysir.

In takaful, however, Shariah professionals monitor and regulate every operational function and process to ensure that each one is in line with the principles of Islamic Shariah. Takaful, therefore, is a much-needed addition to the welfare of a society and its participants. It is a perfect loss-mitigation tool, which can be used by individuals and businesses alike to meet their specific needs.

Let's explain the difference with the help of a case study.

Case Study 3.1 Risk-Sharing Versus Risk-Transfer Mechanism
Person A owns a car worth USD 700,000. They are worried about the financial risk of loss if the car is damaged in an accident or stolen. So, Person A could contact a general insurance company and ask them to insure the car against the risk of damage or theft. They may accept the application and ask for a premium of USD 20,000 in return. In this case, Person A would pay the premium and transfer the risk of financial loss to the insurance company.

Person A works in a company that employs 100 people. For the purposes of simplification, they all own a car worth USD 700,000. The employees fear the same risks, so they may also contact a general insurance company and arrange insurance for their cars by paying premiums of USD 20,000 each. They could all buy insurance and attain peace of mind by transferring the risk of financial loss to the insurer.

But at the same time, although they would attain peace of mind by insuring their cars, they would have used a mechanism that is considered objectionable by most Islamic scholars. Therefore, the employees think about what other options are available.

The employees decide not to pay the USD 20,000 premium to the insurance company for protection against the risk of damage and theft to their cars. By making this decision, they save a total of USD 2 million.

Instead of paying USD 2 million to the insurance company, the employees decide to create their own takaful fund and place the money into that. They agree that if any of their cars is damaged or stolen, the takaful fund will compensate the owner of the car. Here, the risk has not been transferred to any person or any legal entity (as is the case when transferring risk to an insurance company). Instead, the risk is shared by all the employees, who have each contributed USD 20,000 to the takaful fund.

(*continued*)

Case Study 3.1 (continued)

Now, if the participants of the takaful increase from 100 to 1000, 10,000, 100,000 or more, the task of collecting contributions from participants and paying compensation from the takaful fund also becomes a larger one, so experts are needed. So, the participants of the takaful fund decide to hire a company that is experienced in collecting contributions to a takaful fund and arranging compensation payments. The participants decide to pay a fee to the company in exchange for its services. They hire the company to pay compensation from the takaful fund and, if the fund is exhausted, to ask the participants to make further contributions. Therefore, the participants own the takaful fund, while the company only looks after the fund.

There are always three parties in takaful, as follows.

1. The takaful fund
2. Participants of the takaful fund
3. The takaful operator

In this case study, the company hired by the employees performs the functions of the takaful operator. The amount of USD 2 million is the takaful fund, while the 100 employees (car owners) are the participants of the takaful fund. With this arrangement, the 100 employees can have real peace of mind, because they have set up a system in which the takaful fund is there to compensate them if their cars are damaged or stolen and to which there are no objections from Islamic scholars. In fact, the scholars support it because it serves the real spirit of our religion, which is to help those who are in need.

Differences Between Takaful and Insurance

Based on research, Islamic scholars have developed the system of takaful in order to mitigate risk within the Shariah ambit. In this section, we will discuss the differences between takaful and insurance in more detail in order to explain how takaful is a Shariah-compliant mechanism.

Contract

Insurance is a sale and purchase agreement in which a client buys cover (a sum assured) from the insurance company by paying a premium. The sum assured may be the value of a car, a building or an item of equipment (among other things). It may also be the contractual amount that a company has to pay to the client's family if the client dies.

In takaful, there is a contract of tabarru, which means donation. Participants contribute donations to a common fund, which compensates them if any event covered occurs. Therefore, we can say that takaful is a tabarru-based contract, whereas conventional insurance is a contract of compensation (aqd mua'wza). All sale and purchase contracts are aqd mua'wza.

Risk-Mitigation Mechanism

Although takaful and insurance are both risk-mitigation tools, there are differences in how they work. One such difference is that insurance is a risk-transfer mechanism, while takaful is a risk-sharing mechanism.

Riba

As discussed in the previous chapter, both types of riba exist in insurance. The two types of riba are riba al Quran and riba al Hadith.

Riba al Quran does not exist in takaful because all investments are made in Shariah-compliant opportunities with the approval of the takaful operator's Shariah professionals. Therefore, income earned on these investments is also permitted (halal). Because of this, using income earned through permitted investment to pay claims does not raise any objections from Islamic scholars.

Riba al Hadith does not exist in takaful because the contract is one of tabarru. Riba al Hadith exists only in sale and purchase (aqd mua'wadat, commutative) transactions.

Gharar (Uncertainty)

As discussed earlier, insurance is a sale and purchase agreement, so all the Shariah requirements for a valid sale apply. *In addition to other requirements for a valid sale, it is important that the subject matter of the sale is specific and clearly identified.*[3] In insurance, the subject matter is not specific or clearly identified, which renders it non-permissible.

From the Shariah perspective, uncertainty is not allowed in sale and purchase transactions. Insurance is a sale and purchase transaction in which the client buys a sum assured by paying a premium to the insurance company. Uncertainty cannot be eliminated from takaful either. However, the agreement can be changed from one of sale and purchase to a contract of tabarru in which a participant contributes to a common fund (the takaful fund) that is owned by all the participants. Uncertainty in a contract of tabarru is allowed and does not make it objectionable.

Maysir

As mentioned in the previous chapter, the following four conditions are required for an activity to be considered as maysir.

- There is a contract of exchange (aqd mua'wadat) between the parties.
- Under the contract, each party puts its ownership in danger.
- No party has control over the event.
- Each party either loses its property or gains ownership of another party's property.

The contract in takaful is not a contract of exchange (or sale and purchase); it is a contract of tabarru. In takaful, the company does not own the takaful fund. Either it is owned by the takaful participants or its ownership lies with Allah Almighty if the takaful fund is a waqf.

A waqf is an Islamic endowment. *In the context of Islamic insurance, it is when customers' contributions are accumulated in a trust fund by a takaful operator, from which fund the participants are paid compensation in future.*

In light of the earlier discussion, we can say that objection of maysir does not exist in takaful.

Ownership of the Takaful

For the purposes of risk mitigation, a takaful fund is created in which all participants contribute according to the risk they add to the takaful. In the wakalah model of takaful (which is when a takaful operator receives a fee

[3] M.I.A. Usmani, *Meezan Bank's guide to Islamic banking*, p. XX.

in return for the services it provides), the takaful operator manages the takaful fund as an agent or administrator, but the takaful fund is owned by the participants who contribute to it. In conventional insurance, the insurance company owns the takaful fund and any premiums paid into the takaful contribute to the company's income.

Investment

Because there is a time gap between when a contribution is made to the takaful fund and when it has to be used to pay a claim, insurance companies invest the takaful fund in order to earn more income. In takaful companies, all investments are made in permissible areas, which mean the income generated is also permissible. This income is then used to pay participants' claims.

Underwriting Profit

Underwriting is a process that an insurance company follows in order to assess a potential client's eligibility for cover. There is said to be an underwriting profit when the premiums collected come to more than the cost of paying claims. In conventional insurance, this profit belongs to the insurance company. However, in the wakalah model of takaful, this profit is called the surplus and belongs to the takaful fund, which is owned by participants.

Shariah Supervision

A Shariah board or Shariah advisor is an integral part of any takaful arrangement. The Shariah board supervises the activities of the operator from a Shariah perspective. This may include:

- Vetting products
- Checking the Shariah compliance of investments
- Checking the Shariah compliance of distributing the surplus among participants

In conventional insurance, no such supervision takes place and there are no laws governing it.

Chapter Summary

This chapter has focused on the concept of takaful. Takaful practices existed in the Arab world before the era of Islam, and they were not objected to in Islam. The recent practice of takaful emerged in 1979, and there are now more than 300 takaful operators across the globe.

Takaful is a contract of tabarru, while conventional insurance is a sale and purchase transaction. The objections to riba al Hadith, maysir and gharar are valid when a contract is commutative, as it is in conventional insurance. However, they are invalid when a contract is non-commutative and is based on tabarru. Therefore, the objections of riba al Hadith, gharar and maysir do not exist in relation to takaful.

CHAPTER 4

Risk and Its Mitigation Techniques

Abstract This chapter has focused on the concept of risk, which is the probability or threat of damage, injury, liability, loss or any other negative occurrence that is caused by external or internal vulnerabilities and may be avoided through pre-emptive actions. In relation to insurance, three pairs of risk have been discussed: pure and speculative, financial and non-financial, and fundamental and particular. Five risk-management techniques have been explained: avoidance, control, acceptance, transference and sharing. To decide which of these techniques to apply, we first need to identify and analyse the risk. At the end of the chapter, a discussion is provided on the concept of managing risk in Islam. The following examples of risk management in Islam have been mentioned: daman khathar ul tareeq, daman ul darak and aaqila.

Keywords Risk • Risk types • Risk management

After reading this chapter, you should understand:

- The concept of risk
- Types of risk
- Techniques for managing risk
- How risk has been managed in Islam

A. Malik, K. Ullah, *Introduction to Takaful*,
https://doi.org/10.1007/978-981-32-9016-7_4

Introduction

The phenomenon of risk provides the basis for insurance and takaful. Although there are different interpretations of risk, we aim to explore it from the perspective of the possibility of loss that is physically associated with property and life. Such risks can include the possibility of a road accident, a death, a fire in a factory or a mugging, among many others. These risks may result in a cash outflow and place a financial burden on those who are affected. Before going into detail about how we can manage the financial losses that are caused by such events, we need to discuss what risk is and look at some common techniques for managing it.

The Meaning of Risk

Literally, *risk* means a deviation of actual outcomes from expected outcomes. In the context of business, however, it is the probability of a loss, because business is usually carried out with the expectation of earning a profit. It is usually possible to reduce the probability of a risk occurring by employing risk-management techniques, such as insurance and takaful.

When we perform the following activities, we always encounter some risk.

- Crossing a busy road: there is the possibility of having an accident, which could injure or kill us.
- Building house in an area prone to earthquakes: an earthquake could damage or destroy our house.
- Driving a car: we could be in an accident, which could injure us or damage the car.
- Death: when we die, this can result in financial distress for our dependants.

These situations illustrate some of the possibilities of financial loss. A risk represents some sort of uncertainty about the future and the events that could bring financial loss to us.

Classifying Risk

There are several types of risk. However, for the purposes of explaining insurance and takaful, we will discuss only the following categories.

- Pure and speculative risk
- Financial and non-financial risk
- Fundamental and particular risk

Pure and Speculative Risk

Pure risk may or may not result in a loss. For instance, when we drive a car, there might be an accident or there might *not* be an accident, but it is not possible to gain from an accident if it happens. The risks of accidental damage to a car or a robbery at a shop are pure risks, with no possibility of profit. If the accident or robbery occurs, there will be a loss; if it does not occur, there will be no a loss.

Speculative risk is when there is a possibility of gain in addition to a possibility of loss. For case study, investing in the stocks of a company and starting up a new business involve not only the risk of loss but also the opportunity to make a profit or gain.

Insurance and takaful deal with only pure risks, such as death, car theft or fire. They do not cover speculative risks.[1]

Financial and Non-financial Risk

Financial risk can be measured in financial terms; for case study, the theft of a car worth USD 80,000 or a fire causing USD 1 million of damage to factory machinery. The financial losses caused by such incidents can be compensated for through takaful.

Other situations may present risks where the outcome cannot be measured in financial terms. For case study, the breakage of an engagement or a friendship may cause psychological damage, but this cannot be expressed in financial terms.

Takaful and insurance deal with financial risk, not with non-financial risk.

Fundamental and Particular Risk

Fundamental risk affects a larger community and is beyond the control of a single individual.[2] Case studies include earthquakes, famines and hurricanes.

[1] IMS Proschool, *IMS module II: risk management and insurance planning.* [City of publication]: Tata McGraw-Hill Education, 2012.

[2] IMS Proschool, *IMS module II*, p. XX.

Particular risk is risk that is linked to an individual or firm.[3] Case studies include a fire breaking out in a house or a car being stolen. The losses caused by such events are limited to one individual or a small group of individuals.

In principle, insurance and takaful deal with particular risks only. However, some contemporary companies also offer cover for losses caused by events such as earthquakes and hurricanes.

Risk Management

Risk management is a process that we follow to avoid, control, reduce, transfer or share risk.[4] The following techniques can be used to manage risk.

- Risk avoidance
- Risk control
- Risk acceptance
- Risk transference
- Risk sharing

Risk Avoidance

A preferred way of managing risk is to avoid the risk altogether. For case study, we may avoid the risk of flooding if we construct a building in an area that is not next to a watercourse. A person who is employed by a mine-clearance company takes a risk when removing mines. However, they may avoid this risk by getting a job with another company, such as a sports club.

Risk Control

In risk control, we take steps to remove the risk or reduce it as far as possible. For case study, a fire in a factory can result in huge human and financial losses. Fire usually breaks out when three elements are combined: oxygen, heat (flame) and a flammable item. In a factory that produces matches, a fire can start when chemicals get hot; for case study, if the ele-

[3] IMS Proschool, *IMS module II*, p. XX.

[4] G. Dickson & B. Stein, *Risk and insurance*. London: The Chartered Insurance Institute, 2002, Chapter 1, pp. 10–12.

ments come into contact with a burning cigarette. It is not possible to remove oxygen from the environment, but it is possible to keep chemicals in a place where they cannot come into contact with heat or flames. In fuel stations, there is always a risk of fire due to the presence of fuel, which is flammable. In such areas, smoking is forbidden in order to reduce the risk of fire. Installing fire extinguishers, fire alarms and sprinkler systems helps to reduce losses if a fire occurs.

Risk Acceptance

In risk acceptance, we accept the risk and take responsibility for managing its consequences. For case study, some organisations provide medical assistance to their employees if they are hospitalised. Instead of taking out health insurance, they pay their employees' medical expenses direct to the hospital or reimburse the cost of medical to their employees.

Risk Transference

When using this technique, we transfer the financial consequences of the loss to another party, which provides compensation, if the risk occurs. That entity can be an insurance company. For case study, a company may insure its factory against the risk of fire, earthquake and flooding. In doing so, they transfer the risk of financial loss caused by these events to the insurance company. If an insured event occurs and damages the factory, the insurance company must compensate the factory for the loss.

Risk Sharing

With this technique, we all share each other's risks. Cooperative societies and cooperative insurance companies operate on this principle. A cooperative society is established on non-commercial basis by its participants for a definite purpose for providing an agreed service. The joint family system used in some societies is another good case study of risk sharing. Family members cooperate with each other to compensate those who experience a loss. Takaful companies use this technique.

Deciding Which Risk-Management Technique to Use

When making an informed decision about which of the risk-management techniques to use, the following steps are important.

Step 1—Risk Identification

Risk identification is the process of identifying particular risks that may cause harm or loss to the subject matter (for case study, a person's life and health, a car, a building or a machinery). A person is compelled to insure their car if they have identified the risk of loss caused by an accident or theft.

Step 2—Risk Analysis

Risk analysis is the process of assessing the seriousness of a risk (in financial terms) and its likely frequency. For case study, if an organisation approaches an insurance company to arrange cover for 100 vehicles, the insurance company will ask the organisation about previous losses that have occurred in relation to their vehicles. In light of that information, the insurance company will decide whether or not to insure those vehicles and the price (premium) it may need to charge for doing so.

Risk Management in Islam

Islam has always encouraged Muslims to adopt risk-management techniques in different areas, provided that these techniques are within the Shariah ambit.

It is mentioned in the Hadith (the collection of sayings and deeds of the Prophet Muhammad (*SAW*), which provides guidance for Muslims to live by):

> 'O Messenger of Allah! Shall I tie it [the camel] and rely [upon Allah], or leave it loose and rely [upon Allah]?' He said: 'Tie it and rely [upon Allah].'

Some case studies of how risk was managed in Islam in olden times are provided in the following section.

Daman Khathar ul Tareeq

In Arabic, *daman* means guarantee, *khathar* means danger and *tareeq* means way, passage or route.

Merchants used to travel in caravans from one place to another in order to trade. It was not unusual for caravans to be looted; therefore, looting was a risk that merchants had to consider. To manage this risk, a practice was followed where someone would advise the caravan to take a particular route that, in his opinion, was safe. The person who gave this advice always guaranteed that if any looting occurred on his suggested route, he would compensate the caravan for the loss. However, at that time, such a guarantee was always free of charge.[5]

Daman ul Darak

The trading of slaves was once common. Some traders used to guarantee to the buyer that if the slave they were buying was later found to be a free man, they would refund the price.

In this case, the risk was transferred to another entity, which is one of the risk-management techniques described earlier.

Aaqila

Arab tribes used to follow a practice in which if it was proved that a person had murdered someone, the person who had committed the murder had to compensate the victim's family. If the murderer's family did not have enough money, their tribe would compensate the victim's family.

Most of these practices were common before Islam. They were allowed to continue by Prophet Muhammad (PBUH). So, for Muslims, such risk-management techniques are allowed.[6]

Chapter Summary

This chapter has focused on the concept of risk, which is the probability or threat of damage, injury, liability, loss or any other negative occurrence that is caused by external or internal vulnerabilities and may be avoided through pre-emptive actions. In relation to insurance, three pairs of risks have been discussed: pure and speculative, financial and non-financial, and fundamental and particular. Five risk-management techniques have been explained: avoidance, control, acceptance, transference and sharing. To decide which of these techniques to apply, we first need to identify and analyse the risk. At the end of the chapter, a discussion was provided on the concept of managing risk in Islam. The following case studies of risk management in Islam were mentioned: daman khathar ul tareeq, daman ul darak and aaqila.

[5] *Al*-Tamin *al*-Tigari Wa *al*-Badil *al*-Islami Page 226, Dar *al*-Itisam.

[6] A. Ullah, *Takaful kee Shariah Haisiyath*. Karachi: Idarath Ul Maarif Karachi, 2009, p. 62.

CHAPTER 5

Takaful Models

Abstract This chapter has focused on the different takaful models being practised around the globe. These models can be broadly divided into non-profit and for-profit. The non-profit category includes the tawuni (cooperative) model, in which the takaful operator does not get anything in return for providing its services. In for-profit models, the takaful operator can earn a fee or a profit share (or both) in return for the services it provides. For-profit models are based on mudarabah and wakalah models. In the mudarabah model, the operator takes a share of the profit, while in the wakalah model the operator takes a fixed fee and gets nothing from the surplus. The wakalah–mudarabah waqf model is a refined for-profit model based on wakalah and is mainly practised in Pakistan. In this model, the takaful fund is declared as a waqf fund and the operator becomes the wakeel. The waqf fund compensates participants for their defined losses when an event that is covered occurs.

Keywords Mudarabah model • Takaful models • Tawuni model • Wakalah model

A. Malik, K. Ullah, *Introduction to Takaful*,
https://doi.org/10.1007/978-981-32-9016-7_5

After reading this chapter, you should understand:

- The role of participants, the takaful fund and the takaful company
- The different models of takaful being practised in different parts of the world

Introduction

Takaful companies operating in different parts of the world have adopted different models in order to offer their services. These models are derived from different forms of Islamic muamalat (Islamic finance), observing the rules and regulations of Islamic law. In Malaysia, the mudarabah and wakalah models are practised, while in the Middle East, the wakalah model is in practice. In Pakistan and South Africa, a mix of the wakalah–waqf and mudarabah models is used. In this chapter, we will discuss these models with special emphasis on the wakalah–waqf model being practised in Pakistan.

Tawuni (Cooperative) Model

The tawuni model can also be called the cooperative model, as it is based on the concept of brotherhood and solidarity among participants of a common fund. A group of people establishes a common fund in which every participant contributes according to the risk that they add to the fund. The cover to be provided by the fund is mutually decided upon by the participants and may include life, motor and property cover for defined risks. Professionals or a company may be engaged to operate the fund, collecting contributions from participants and paying compensation when a defined loss occurs. The professionals or company is not paid any compensation for the services they provide: the surplus is distributed among the participants. Therefore, this model is also called a non-profit model. This concept was practised by the first takaful operator, which was established in 1979 in Sudan.

For-Profit Takaful Models

In addition to the tawuni (non-profit) model, other models have been developed that retain the provisions of compensation and profit for the takaful service providers. These models are based on different contracts of Islamic muamalat, including wakalah, mudarabah and waqf contracts.

Wakalah Model

In Arabic, *wakeel* means agent. The term wakalah is used in Islamic finance to describe a contract of agency or delegated authority under which the muwakkil (principal) appoints a wakeel (agent) to carry out a specific task on its behalf. Several takaful models are based on this agent–principal relationship.

In the wakalah model, the takaful fund is the principal. The takaful fund appoints a takaful company as a wakeel to provide various services. Because the takaful company only operates the takaful fund, it is also called the takaful operator.

Pure Wakalah

In the pure wakalah model, the takaful operator is the wakeel and the takaful fund is the principal. In practice, nowadays, the takaful fund is created by the operator, although theoretically it should be created by the takaful participants. After creating the takaful fund, the operator invites people to become participants of that fund. The takaful fund provides different types of risk protection in return for a specified contribution (similar to risk charge or premium in conventional insurance).

People can become participants of the fund if they contribute a specific amount to the fund for a defined type of cover. Each person's contribution is calculated based on the type and amount of cover that they have requested. Their contribution is paid into the takaful fund. As part of operating the takaful fund, the operator decides whether or not the cover requested by the client should be provided and, if so, the extent of the cover and the contribution needed from the client.

The takaful operator (as wakeel or agent) performs the following activities:

- Collecting contributions from participants.
- Placing contributions into the takaful fund.
- Investing money from the takaful fund.
- Paying compensation to participants from the takaful fund if any covered event occurs.
- If the money in the takaful fund is used up, may ask the participants to make more contributions.
- If there is any money left in the takaful fund after paying participants' claims, distributing the surplus among participants who have not made a claim.

In return for providing these services, the takaful operator is compensated in the form of a wakalah fee (a service fee), which is always a percentage of the total contributions made to the takaful fund.

All these functions need to be performed by a team of professionals and should be offered through a properly registered and regulated company. The services of these companies should be monitored by the regulator. For these reasons, only licensed takaful operators are allowed to invite clients to become participants of a takaful fund. The regulator grants licences only to takaful operators that meet the following conditions. To be licensed, the company must:

- Meet the minimum requirement for paid-up capital
- Appoint a board of directors
- Have a structure of Shariah governance
- Set up the takaful fund
- Develop products
- Have specific administrative processes in place

One or more shareholders must arrange for all the requirements of the regulator to be met and apply for the licence. After getting the licence, the company invites people to become participants of the takaful fund through contributions in return for the type and extent of cover they want. Here, the relationship between the takaful operator and the takaful fund is one of wakeel–muwakkil in which the operator is the wakeel and the takaful fund is the muwakkil.

Throughout the year, the operator processes claims and pays them out of the takaful fund. At the end of the year, after paying all the claims, if anything is left in the takaful fund, it belongs in full to the takaful fund; that is, the participants. In conventional insurance, if anything remains in the takaful fund, it belongs to the insurance company. In the pure wakalah model, the operator cannot receive any part of the surplus.

A deficit may occur if the total cost of claims exceeds the total contributions made. In this case, the participants should be asked to contribute more into the takaful fund. However, in practice, this is not a viable option, as it is always difficult to ask participants to make further contributions in the middle of the year. Therefore, a more viable option

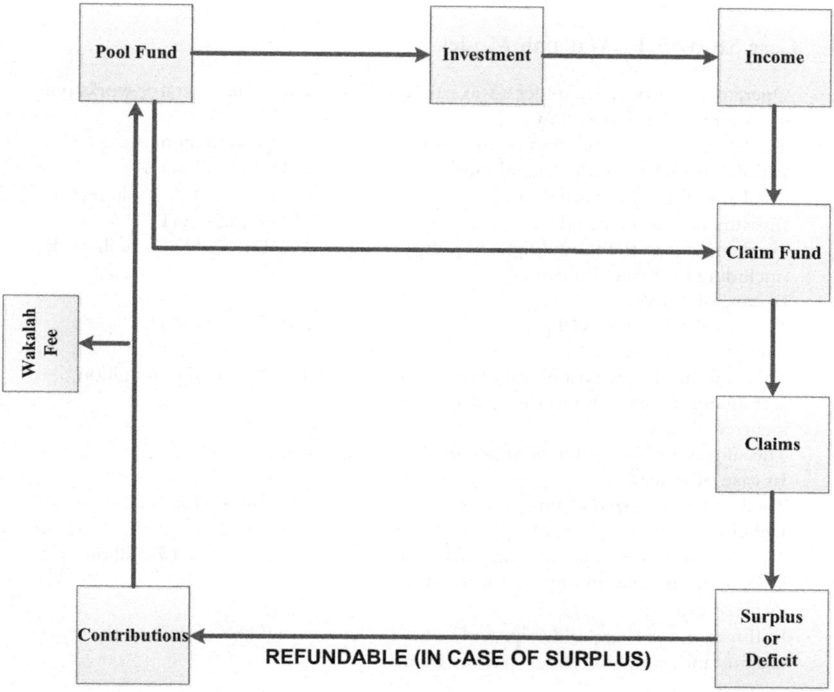

Fig. 5.1 A simplified wakalah model

is practised in which, if there is a deficit, the company shareholders provide a qard-e-hasna (an interest-free loan) to the takaful fund, which is used to pay claims. Every shareholder provides a share of the qard-e-hasna in accordance with the size of their share in the takaful operator. If any surplus occurs in the future, it is first used to pay the qard-e-hasna.

The wakalah takaful model (Fig. 5.1) has been simplified and is displayed for the purpose of aiding students' understanding. In reality, the model is far more detailed and complex.

This model is in practice in Middle Eastern countries (Fig. 5.1).

Let's look at the working of the wakalah model using a case study.

Case Study 5.1 Wakalah Model

Operator A is operating under a wakalah model of takaful. The operator works out its surplus / deficit as follows.

Total contributions collected by the operator:	USD 100 million (A)
Wakalah fee @25% of the takaful fund:	USD 25 million (B)
Total amount in the takaful fund:	A – B = USD 75 million (C)
Investment income earned:	USD 8 million (D)
Total amount in the takaful fund (including investment income):	(C + D) = USD 83 million (E)
In case of surplus	
Total cost of incurred claims:	USD 70 million (F)
Surplus:	
Total amount in the takaful fund (including investment income) minus the total cost of incurred claims:	(E – F) = USD 13 million

The surplus of USD 13 million belongs to the participants in full.

In case of deficit	
Total cost of incurred claims:	USD 90 million (G)
Deficit:	
Total amount in the takaful fund (including investment income) minus total amount of incurred claims:	(E – G) = USD 7 million

In this case, the shareholders provide a qard-e-hasna of USD 7 million to the takaful fund, which is used to pay the claims.

The Pure Wakalah Model in Family Takaful

The pure wakalah model used in family takaful is the basic structure of the wakalah model. We will go through the model step by step, assessing what happens at each stage of the process.

It is important to note that all relations between the takaful operator and the participants are based on the wakalah contract. The takaful operator is the wakeel, who acts on behalf of the participants in underwriting and investment. The role of a takaful operator is to manage all the affairs of the takaful in return for a predetermined fee, which is called the wakalah fee.

1. The participant contributes under the scheme.

As mentioned previously, the amount given by the participants into takaful fund is called contributions, not premiums. This is because they are based on the concept of tabarru, contribution, donations. Rather than purchasing cover in exchange for premiums, participants donate money to a risk takaful out of which claims are paid to other contributors. However, the donor wants cover that is Shariah-compliant. Therefore, his donation may be described as being conditional. The result is a conditional donation, which conforms to Shariah; takaful participants donate a sum of money to a risk takaful subject to the condition that they will receive compensation from the takaful for specific types of loss.

2. The contribution is divided into:
   - A contribution towards the wakalah fee
   - An amount to be placed into the participants' investment account
   - An amount to be placed into the participants' risk account

In family takaful, which is the alternative to life insurance, after taking an amount for the wakalah fee participants' contributions are further divided into a risk account and an investment account. The return from the investment account is not part of the mutual risk cover. It is invested in order to build up wealth for participants who survive the term or for their beneficiaries if they die.

The wakalah fee is paid upfront to the takaful operator out of the initial contributions. The takaful operator manages the risk account and the investment account; however, the wakalah fee covers managing the risk account only, which is used for paying the death claims. The wakalah fee must cover all the management costs (not including the cost of claims and the direct cost of handling claims) in addition to shareholder profit. The wakalah fee is invested, and profits on it are enjoyed only by the takaful operator. The takaful operator also takes a share of the profit generated from investing the fund. This share is a fixed percentage, not a fixed amount.

The wakalah fee includes a fee for managing the underwriting. This is taken from the participants' risk account. In addition, there is a wakalaht ul istismar, which is an agency contract for the use of assets. The operator provides fee for the investment management services. This fee is paid from the participants' investment account.

3. The money from the investment and risk accounts is invested in Shariah-compliant investments.
4. Any profit earned from the investments is added back to the respective accounts.

One important reason that takaful is lawful from the perspective of Shariah is that the money contributed by participants is invested in Shariah-compliant investments. No investments that can bear interest (riba) are considered by the takaful operator. All investments are interest-free. The profit from investing the contributions is then added to the respective accounts.

The takaful operator always takes care to make sure that the funds in the participants' investment account and the participants' risk account stay separate. The takaful operator manages them separately, even if money from the accounts is invested in the same instrument.

5. The money in the participants' risk account is used to pay claims, pay re-takaful fees and create reserves. (Re-takaful is takaful cover taken out by takaful companies for better management of risk.) The money in the participants' investment account is accumulated and paid to participants (or their beneficiaries) if they die, if they surrender (leave the scheme) or when the scheme matures.
6. The money left over in the participants' risk account is called the surplus.

Only the money in the participants' risk account is used to pay claims, pay re-takaful fees or create reserves. Any money left over after this is known as the surplus. If the claims, re-takaful fees and reserves are in excess of the total contributions made by the participants, the fund runs into a deficit.

7. If there is a surplus, it is shared among the participants.

The surplus is paid back to participants in the same proportion as they paid their contributions. Since this is the money left over from their contribution payments and investment income, it is paid back to them after all the necessary claims have been paid.

8. The shareholders use the wakalah fee to cover their operating expenses.
9. If there is a deficit in the participants' risk account, the shareholders provide a qard-e-hasna to cover any immediate claims. The loan has to be interest-free to make it Shariah-compliant.

The loan provided by the takaful operator to cover the deficit has to be paid back. This is done using future surpluses in the participants' risk account. The ultimate obligation to pay claims lies with the takaful fund, which is owned by the participants—the takaful operator provides a loan only to fill an immediate gap in funding.

Modified Wakalah with a Performance Fee

This model differs slightly from the pure wakalah model as follows. When there is a surplus, the takaful operator, as the wakeel of the takaful fund, is given an agreed share of the surplus in addition to the wakalah fee. Sharing the surplus gives the takaful operator an incentive to carry out sound underwriting and investment of the takaful fund.

Mudarabah Model

The mudarabah model is based on a type of partnership in Islamic business in which:

- One business partner provides the capital and is called the rab ul maal (the capital owner).
- The other provides the skill and is called the mudarib (the skills provider).

If there is a profit, the partners divide this between them in accordance with previously agreed shares. If there is a loss, the rab ul maal has to bear this, and the mudarib does not get anything for the skills and services they have provided.

The following takaful models are based on mudarabah.

Pure Mudarabah

The pure mudarabah model (Fig. 5.2) was introduced in Malaysia after the Takaful Act came into force in 1984. In this model, at the start of their relationship, the participants of the takaful fund and the takaful operator

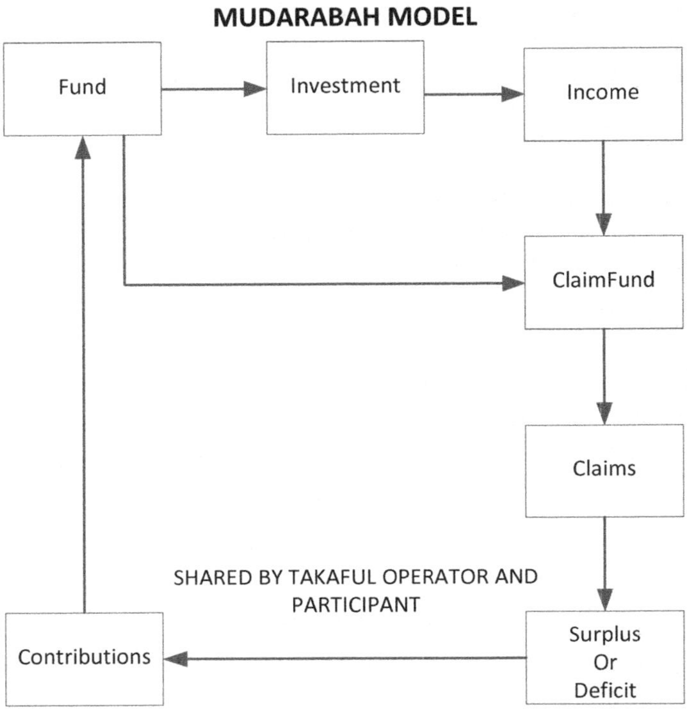

Fig. 5.2 Mudarabah takaful model

enter into a mudarabah contract, which sets out what protection is offered and in what ratio the underwriting results will be shared. The surplus (that is, the profit) is shared between the participants and the takaful operator in line with this agreed ratio. This model allows the takaful operator to share in profits resulting from underwriting activities in addition to sharing good returns on invested premiums.

This model is currently practised in Malaysia.

Throughout the year, the operator processes claims and pays them out of the fund. At the end of the year, after paying all the claims, if anything is left in the fund, it is the profit and is shared between the operator and the participants in the agreed ratio. In conventional insurance, if anything remains in the fund, it belongs to the insurance company.

A loss may occur if the total cost of claims exceeds the total contributions made. In this case, the participants should be asked to contribute more into the fund. However, in practice, this is not a viable option, as it is always difficult to ask participants to make further contributions in the middle of the year. Therefore, a more viable option is practised in which, if there is a deficit, the company shareholders provide a qard-e-hasna (an interest-free loan) to the fund, which is used to pay claims. Every shareholder provides a share of the qard-e-hasna in accordance with the size of their share in the takaful operator. If any profit occurs in the future, it is first used to payback the qard-e-hasna.

Wakalah–Mudarabah Model

This model is a combination of the wakalah and mudarabah models. In this model, the takaful operator is compensated for the following services in the form of a wakalah fee, which is paid upfront.

1. Collecting contributions from participants.
2. Placing contributions into the takaful fund.
3. Paying compensation from the takaful fund if a participant suffers a defined loss.
4. If the fund is exhausted, asking participants to make further contributions.
5. If there is a surplus in the fund after all claims have been paid, distributing this among participants.

The takaful operator invests the takaful fund on a mudarabah basis. Here, the takaful fund is the rab ul maal, while the takaful operator is the mudarib. The profit earned on this investment is divided between both partners—the takaful operator and the mudarib—in a predetermined ratio.

Let's explain this with the help of a case study.

Case Study 5.2

Total contributions collected by the operator:	USD 100 million (A)
Wakalah fee @25% of the takaful fund:	USD 25 million (B)
Total left in the takaful fund:	(A – B) = USD 75 million (C)
Investment income earned:	USD 8 million (D)
Profit ratio:	25% to the takaful operator and 75% to the takaful fund

(*continued*)

Case Study 5.2 (continued)

Takaful fund's share:	75% of USD 8 million = USD 6 million (E)
Total amount in the takaful fund, including profit:	(C + E) = USD 81 million (F)
In Case of Surplus	
Total incurred claims:	USD 70 million (G)
Surplus:	(F − G) = 81 − 70 = USD 11 million
The surplus of USD 11 million belongs to the participants.	
In Case of Deficit	
Total incurred claims:	USD 90 million (H)
Deficit:	(F − H) = 81 − 90 = PRK −9 million

The shareholders of the takaful operator provide a qard-e-hasna of USD 9 million to the takaful fund, which is used to pay the claims.

Wakalah–Mudarabah Waqf Model

Before we look at the details of the wakalah–mudarabah waqf model, let's explain waqf.

Waqf

The literal meaning of the word waqf is confinement, detention, holding and prohibition. *In Islamic finance, a waqf is an endowment or charity institution to which participants contribute valuables for a specific cause.*[1] It involves assigning the benefits of use of non-consumable property to designated beneficiaries. Non-consumable property can be buildings or vehicles but not, for case study, cement or wood, which are consumed.

A waqf is a legal entity that can hold or dispose of property and can sue and can be sued.

The concept of a waqf is based on the saying of Prophet Muhammad (PBUH):

> when a child of Adam dies, his chapter of deeds is closed forever except for three, for [one who founded] a perpetual charity during his lifetime, [a scholar who left behind him] a legacy of knowledge that benefits people at large, and a pious child of the deceased who constantly seeks Allah's mercy for him. (Muslim, Hadith: 1631)

[1] K. Ullah, *Adaptable service-system design: an analysis of Shariah finance in Pakistan*. PhD thesis, Brunel University Business School, 2014, p. XX.

A waqf can be considered as a long-term charitable donation because it is perpetual in nature. A waqf deed mentions the property, the waqif (the person donating the use of the property), the mutawalli (the waqf administrator) and the beneficiaries.

There are three types of waqf: waqf ahli, waqf kahiri and waqf mushtarak.

Waqf Ahli

A waqf ahli is a waqf that is intended to support the children of the waqif (the waqf creator). For case study, the waqif can declare a building as a waqf to support his or her children. The children cannot sell the building, but they will get the income generated from that building—for case study, from rent.

Waqf Khairi

A waqf khairi is a philanthropic waqf. It is used to provide general welfare for both religious and non-religious purposes. It includes financing mosques and educational institutions. It is also used to help people in need.

Waqf Mushtarak

A waqf mushtarak is used to help charities and individuals. Part of the income generated by the property declared as waqf mushtarak can be given to individuals (for case study, the waqif's children), and part can be given to charitable institutions (for case study, a hospital being run on a welfare basis that provides cost-free or subsidised treatment to patients).

Now that we have explained waqf, we can return to the wakalah–mudarabah waqf model.

The Wakalah–Mudarabah Waqf Takaful Model

This model is similar to the wakalah model. The only difference is that takaful fund is given the status of a waqf fund.

The wakalah–mudarabah waqf model was developed to respond to criticisms of earlier models. In order to develop the takaful system on a welfare basis and ensure its continuity, while developing the Takaful Rules in Pakistan in 2005, Mufti Muhammad Taqi Usmani suggested declaring the takaful fund to be a waqf fund. This was approved by the Securities and Exchange Commission, the takaful regulator in Pakistan, in its Takaful Rules (2005). According to these rules, wakalah–mudarabah waqf is the only takaful model that can be practised in Pakistan.

In this model, the shareholders of the takaful operator establish a waqf fund by contributing a seed amount (part of the capital) and inviting people to become participants. A waqf deed defines the cover that the waqf fund will provide to its participants. The waqf deed is developed by the waqif, which, in this context, is the takaful operator. The dual role of takaful company as operator as well as developer of waqf deed may result into agency problem where it may allow excessive risks to the waqf fund in order to earn more and more wakalah fee.

People can become participants by filling in a proposal form with information about the cover they need and other details the takaful operator requires. The operator's underwriter evaluates the information provided by the applicant. If the applicant's risk profile is within a range that is acceptable to the fund, the takaful operator enrols them as a participant of the waqf fund. The new participant then contributes. The takaful operator receives its wakalah fee out of the contributions paid by each participant of the waqf fund. General takaful companies in Pakistan use the wakalah–waqf model displayed in Fig. 5.3.

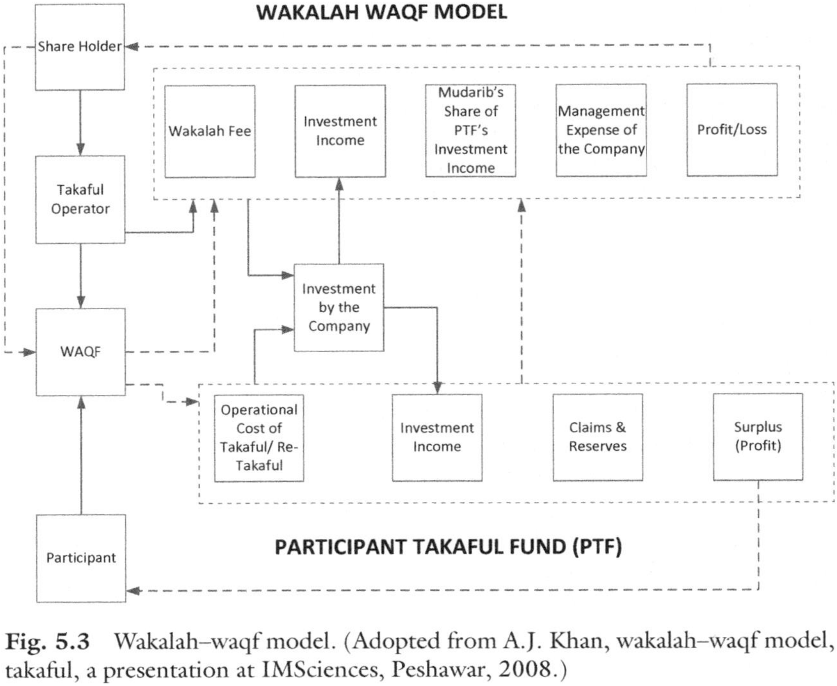

Fig. 5.3 Wakalah–waqf model. (Adopted from A.J. Khan, wakalah–waqf model, takaful, a presentation at IMSciences, Peshawar, 2008.)

As discussed earlier, in family takaful, the rest of the contribution is divided into two accounts.

- Participants' investment account
- Participants' risk account

If a loss occurs that is covered by the waqf fund, the participant or their beneficiary is compensated from the risk account. The investment portion, along with any profit, is paid from the investment account.

There are three parties in the wakalah–mudarabah waqf model.

- The waqf fund
- The participants of the waqf fund
- The takaful operator

The Waqf Fund

The waqf fund is created by the takaful operator (the waqif) by contributing a seed amount. This money remains in the fund and cannot be spent.

The waqf fund has the following objectives:

- To give financial assistance to its participants in the event of loss.
- To extend benefits to its participants in line with the waqf deed.

The waqf fund lays down the rules for how its funds are distributed to the beneficiaries and decides how much compensation should be given to a participant when a defined loss occurs. The waqf fund is the owner of all contributions to the fund and has the right to act as a legal entity in accordance with its terms for investing, paying compensation and dealing with any surplus. (Presently, these waqf rules are developed by the takaful operator, although there is some debate about who should develop these rules: the takaful operator is an agent of the takaful fund, and when the agent develops rules for the principal, this raises concerns.)

With approval from the takaful operator's Shariah board, the surplus may be distributed as follows:

- One portion of the surplus should be kept in reserve to mitigate future losses.
- Another portion should be distributed among participants of the fund.

- Another portion may be given to charity, subject to the approval of the Shariah board.

The Takaful Operator

As the manager of the waqf fund, the takaful operator performs the following functions, which are necessary for the fund to operate. In return, the operator is paid a wakalah fee from the waqf fund.

- *Sound Underwriting*

The takaful operator must perform sound underwriting of the risks being added to the waqf fund. The underwriter has to accept those risks that are within the acceptable range for the waqf. In family takaful operators, the underwriter checks the profile of the applicant, considering their age, health, financial status and other relevant factors. In general takaful, in the case of risks relating to a car, the underwriter has to check the fame of the applicant in terms of credibility, their driving history, the value of the car and so on. If the applicant's risk is found to be within the acceptable range, the takaful operator will set a contribution amount based on the applicant's risk profile. The applicant becomes a participant of the waqf fund once they have made a contribution to the fund.

- *Paying Genuine Claims*

The takaful operator is responsible for confirming that participants' claims are genuine and then paying compensation promptly. The operator has the right to investigate claims to confirm that they are true.

- *Investing the Fund*

As the mudarib of the fund, the takaful operator manages the investment of excess waqf funds in Shariah-compliant investments. The operator takes a predetermined share of any profit from the fund's investments. This model was developed in Pakistan and was adopted in the Takaful Rules 2005 developed by the Securities Exchange Commission of Pakistan, which regulates insurance and takaful companies in Pakistan.

- *Refunding Any Surplus*

You may be asking the following question: can participants claim a refund for an amount they have donated to a waqf fund?

Here is the answer. The amount that is considered to be a waqf is the seed money that was initially deposited in the fund by the shareholders of the takaful operator from the operator's paid-up capital. This money cannot be consumed, even to pay participants' claims. However, participants' contributions are not part of the waqf; instead, they are the mamlook (property) of the waqf. Therefore, participants' claims can be paid from the money contributed by participants.

For example, consider that someone donates land for the purpose of welfare, such as building a school, college, orphanage or mosque. That waqf (donation) cannot be taken back, because the ownership passes to Allah Almighty. However, any amount donated to, for case study, the school or mosque built on the waqf land does not become part of the waqf itself but is owned by the waqf. When we donate an amount to a mosque, it can be used to pay the expenses of the mosque, such as utility (electricity, gas and phone) bills. In the same way, participants' claims can be paid from the waqf fund in line with the waqf deed. If anything remains in the fund after the claims have been paid, it can be refunded to the participants.

The takaful business models used by Pak–Qatar general and family takaful companies are displayed in Exhibits 5.1 and 5.2, respectively.

Differences Between Takaful Models

Table 5.1 sets out the main differences between the takaful models explained in this chapter.

Refined Takaful Model

The wakalah–mudarabah waqf model is considered to be a refined takaful model. Because of the presence of the waqf, it has the benefit of welfare: participants contribute to the waqf fund in order to pay each other compensation when losses occur. Declaring the takaful fund a waqf fund increases its protection, sustainability and transparency further, as it is more difficult for the operator to withdraw money from the waqf fund to pay its own expenses. Because the takaful fund is a waqf fund, making decisions about distributing any surplus becomes easy.

TAKAFUL BUSINESS MODEL: GENERAL

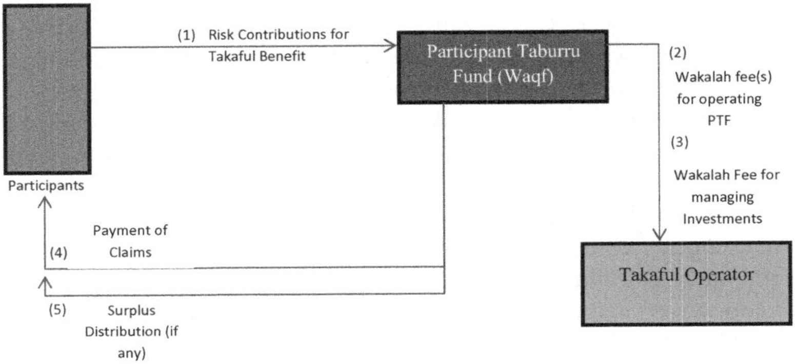

PARTIES INVOLVED

TITLE	DESCRIPTION
Participants	- Participants can be individuals or a company - Participants pay Risk Contributions as per the Takaful Plan they have applied for to become members of the PTF. - On membership, they become entitled to the benefits as described in the Participant Membership Document (PMD) of the said Takaful Plan
Participant Taburru Fund (PTF) – Waqf	- PTF means Pak-Qatar General Takaful Limited established under the Waqf Settlement Deed
Takaful Operator (TO)	- Takaful Operator or Trustee means Pak-Qatar General Takaful Limited is working in its capacity as Wakeel thereby operating the PTF - The terms Operator or Trustee may be used interchangeably

RELATIONSHIP BETWEEN THE PARTIES INVOLVED

Participants have no relationship with the Takaful Operator at any stage of the business operation. The Takaful Operator creates the PTF by ceding Waqf amount. It is on behalf of the Waqf that the Operator nominates itself as the Wakeel

Exhibit 5.1 General takaful model

PROCESS FLOW

1. **Risk Contributions for Takaful Benefits**
   Risk Contribution is pooled into the Participant Taburru Fund (PTF) which is based on Waqf
   - Net Contribution for each Participant is calculated as follows:
     Takaful Contributions received in the PTF
     Less: Change in Technical Reserves
     Less: Earned Portion of Takaful Operator's Fee
     Less: Incurred Claims
   - Risk Contribution is treated as Taburru. Taburru relinquishes all ownership rights of the Participant on the amount and performs the crucial role of eliminating Riba and rendering Gharar and Qimar ineffective from the contract
   - Risk Contribution once pooled into the PTF is regarded as the property of Waqf

2. **Wakalah Fee for Operating PTF and Managing Investments**
   From the PTF, the Operator deducts the Wakalah Fee for Operating the PTF and Wakalatul-Istismar Fee/Modaraba Profit for managing investments in the PTF on behalf of the PTF

3. **Payment of Claims**
   - Participant notifies the Operator in writing about the loss or damage giving an indication as to its nature and extent and lodges a claim,
   - Claim is paid from the PTF

4. **Surplus Distribution**
   - Surplus is unique to Takaful business
   - In case the net Contribution for the Participant is negative, no surplus would be paid to that Participant
   - In case there is a deficit in the PTF, the Takaful Operator will donate an interest-free loan to be called Qard-e-Hasana to make good the shortfall in the fund. The loan shall be repaid from the future surpluses generated in the PTF

PARTICIPANT TAKAFUL FUND (PTF)

PTF is a separate and independent entity capable of having title to ownership of, and possession of assets whether in the form of moneys, movable and immovable properties, and/or in any other tangible or intangible form legally possible and permissible along with the compliance with the Shariah principles.

The objects and purposes of the PTF are as follows:

1. To receive contributions, donations, gifts, charities, subscriptions etc., from the Participants and others;
2. To provide relief to the Participants against benefits defined as per the PTF Rules, the PMD and any Takaful Supplementary Benefit Document(s);
3. To give charities in consultation with the Shariah Board;
4. To invest monies of the PTF in and subscribe for, take, acquire, trade or deal in, instruments approved by the Shariah Board such as shares, stocks, sukuk, bonds, securities or investments of redeemable capital of any other company, institution, mutual fund, corporation or body corporate or any other manner;
5. To do all such other things/acts/objects as are incidental or conducive to the attainment of the above objects or any of them

Exhibit 5.1 (continued)

The Takaful Operator has set apart Rupees Five hundred thousand only (Rs. 500,000) and ceded the same to the PTF being the Waqf money;

Assets of the PTF

1. The cede amount donated from the SHF to the PTF
2. The risk contributions and the Takaful Operator's Fee received from the Participants by way of subscriptions, contributions, donations, gifts, etc; and
3. Income or incomes derived from investments etc. made by the PTF except for the ceding amount (referred to as above) all the balance amounts may be utilized for offsetting the PTF's liabilities of payments of benefits to the members of the Fund

The Takaful Operator may require such technical reserves to be set up in the PTF, as may be deemed appropriate, that is to say:

1. Unearned contributions reserves
2. Incurred but not reported claims' reserve
3. Deficiency reserve
4. Reserve for Qard-e-Hasana to be returned in the future; and
5. Surplus equalization reserve

SOURCES OF REVENUE – Takaful Operator

PTF is the only source of revenue for the Takaful Operator.

1. **Wakalah Fee for Operating the PTF**
   The Operator deducts 'Wakalah Fee' for operating the PTF. The Roles and Responsibilities of the Operator are described in the Waqf Deed Clause 4 and 5

2. **Wakalatul Istismar Fee or Modaraba Profit**
   The Operator may either charge a fixed Wakalatul Istismar Fee from or earn a profit share in a Modaraba agreement with the PTF as part of investment management services rendered. Modarib's Share in the investment could be 40%

Exhibit 5.1 (continued)

Chapter Summary

This chapter has focused on the different takaful models being practised around the globe. These models can be broadly divided into non-profit and for-profit.

The non-profit category includes the tawuni (cooperative) model, in which the takaful operator does not get anything in return for providing its services.

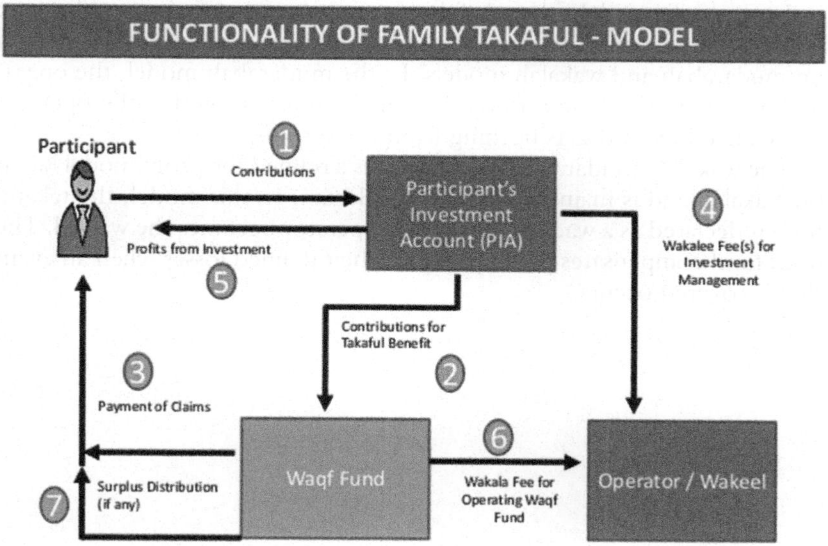

Exhibit 5.2 Family takaful model

Table 5.1 Differences between takaful models

	Feature	*Takaful models*			
		Tawuni	Wakalah	Wakalah–mudarabah waqf	Mudarabah
1	Operator's earnings	No earnings	Wakalah fee only	Wakalah fee and share in the investment profit as mudarib	Share in the profit (surplus) only
2	Ownership of takaful fund	Participants	Participants	Waqf	Business
3	Ownership of surplus	Participants	Participants	As decided by the waqf (but the operator has no share in it)	Shared between participants and the operator

In for-profit models, the takaful operator can earn a fee or a profit share (or both) in return for the services it provides. For-profit models are based on mudarabah and wakalah models. In the mudarabah model, the operator takes a share of the profit, while in the wakalah model, the operator takes a fixed fee and gets nothing from the surplus.

The wakalah–mudarabah waqf model is a refined for-profit model based on wakalah and is mainly practised in Pakistan. In this model, the takaful fund is declared as a waqf fund, and the operator becomes the wakeel. The waqf fund compensates participants for their defined losses when an event that is covered occurs.

CHAPTER 6

Family Takaful

Abstract This chapter has focused on the different services that family takaful companies offer. These services can be divided into unit-linked family takaful and family-term takaful. Unit-linked family takaful pays compensation to beneficiaries if a participant dies or becomes disabled and has a saving element if a participant survives the coverage duration. Family-term takaful provides only death benefit. Basic cover can be expanded by adding appropriate supplementary clauses to the contract. In family takaful, supplementary clauses, such as accidental death and dismemberment (AD&D) or an annuity, can be added to the basic contract.

Keywords Family takaful • Family-term takaful • Unit-linked family takaful

After reading this chapter, you should understand:

- Family, general and supplementary benefits (riders)
- Generic plans of family takaful
- Unit pricing methodology
- Supplementary contracts (riders)

A. Malik, K. Ullah, *Introduction to Takaful*,
https://doi.org/10.1007/978-981-32-9016-7_6

Introduction

In the modern world, takaful has entered every sphere of life and business. You can cover your life, health and property, such as your home, furniture and fixtures, and electronic appliances. In business, you can cover your factory buildings, machinery, vehicles, physical stock, goods and cash in transit, and employers' liability, among others. Anything of value or that generates income for a person can be covered against some risk. For these and many other types of covers, takaful companies have developed a range of products that cater to customers' needs. In this chapter, we will study these products in detail.

Takaful products can be divided into three broad categories or classes.

1. Family (life)
2. General (non-life)
3. Health

Family Takaful

In this chapter, we will focus on family takaful. Family takaful provides financial compensation if the person who is covered dies or becomes disabled. In family takaful, every participant nominates a beneficiary when they join the takaful fund (waqf fund). If a participant dies, the face value or cash value of units, whichever is higher, is paid to the participant's beneficiary.

The beneficiary must be someone who would suffer a loss if the participant died. Usually, this is established by the relationship. For example, a wife has an interest in the life of her husband, and a son and daughter have an interest in the life of their father. If the beneficiary is a child, the participant also appoints a guardian.

Family takaful cover can be arranged to protect beneficiaries against financial loss caused by any of the following happenings to the participant:

- Death
- Disability
- Illness

The amount paid to on death or maturity of cover by a family takaful operator is used to meet short-term and long-term needs, such as:

- Paying for children's education and weddings
- Buying a new house
- Paying Hajj or Umrah expenses
- Income for retirement

There are two main types of family takaful: unit-linked and term life.

Unit-Linked Family Takaful

Universal life takaful provides death cover and a savings arrangement. It is arranged for a multiple number of years, and participants make the decided annual contribution in order to remain covered for the face value and profit, if any. Universal life is a type of cover that generates savings for the client if he or she is still alive when the membership matures.

In the universal life coverage, a takaful company invests the collected contribution and earns money through the investments. A portion of earned money is shared with the clients as profit and is paid on death or maturity of the contract. There are two system of profit sharing with the clients, namely, bonus-linked and unit-linked profit-sharing systems.

Bonus-Linked Profit-Sharing System

After year end, the company works out the cash inflows like collected contribution, investment income, and cash outflows like claims paid, administrative expenses and taxes and arrives on the net profit earned. A portion of that profit is distributed among shareholders of the company in the form of dividends, and some of it is retained as earnings and reserves creation for future claims. A portion of total profit shared among the policyholders through a rate per 1000 of sum covered/face value is declared. For instance, consider a client who has a coverage of USD 40,000 and a rate of USD 10 per USD 1000 is announced, then the client will get USD 400 (10 × 40) bonus for that year. USD 400 bonus will be credited to the client's contract number. Each year, when the client pays the contribution, a bonus rate is announced, and the bonus accumulates. Accumulated bonuses are paid in full in only two cases: either on death or on maturity. If someone cancels the contract, then a discounted value of sum assured and accumulated bonuses is paid. It is a relatively conventional system, and very few companies practise it.

Case Study 6.1 Maturity Claim
Arnold takes a family takaful plan for savings and protection against the risk of financial loss if he dies. Details are as under:

Sum assured: USD 50,000

Duration of cover: 20 years

Annual contribution: USD 1800

The company follows bonus-based system for profit distribution system. After one year, the company finalises accounts and declares bonus rates of USD 20 per 1000 of sum assured for the clients.

Number of 1000s in sum assured = 50

Bonus rate per 1000 = 20

Annual bonus for Arnold's contract = Bonus rate × Number of 1000s in sum assured

=20 × 50 = USD 1000

In the following years, bonus rate may change depending on the company's performance. Each year, Arnold pays annual contribution, and bonus credits to his contract when the year ends.

Arnold dies in a road traffic accident after paying six annual contributions. In six years, six bonuses are credited to Arnold's takaful account amounting USD 10,000.

Being beneficiary, Mary, Arnold's widow, claims for the death proceeds. The company pays the claim as follows:

Sum assured = USD 50,000

Bonus = USD 10,00

Total death claim = USD 60,000

Unit-Linked Profit Distribution System

In this system, contribution paid by the client is deposited into two accounts: waqf (risk) account and investment account.

Waqf Fund

In takaful, waqf fund is maintained for the risk management, while in conventional insurance companies, the same objective is achieved through an account called risk account and is owned by the company; in takaful, the takaful company works as manager of the waqf fund and does not own it. Companies following waqf fund system also invest the collected contribution and earn profit on it. They pool it in a fund called investment account. A portion of the annual contribution is calculated based on mortality (to pay death claims) and is added to the risk account also called takaful fund. If the participant dies, the face value is paid out of the takaful fund, which is the participants' risk account, and is used only to pay death claims and other covered events like disability. It is also called the participant takaful fund (PTF). The contribution that a participant has to make to this fund depends on:

- The entry age
- The amount of cover they apply for

As age increases, so does the mortality rate, which results in a corresponding increase in the contribution. It may also increase if the participant is engaged in a profession transferring more than a normal risk to takaful fund. Such professions can be working in an atomic reactor, police job, manual staff of a construction company that builds high-rise buildings, driving, demining firm and so forth. The contribution may also increase if the participant is having some health problem that increases the risk of dying earlier within the same age group. The health problem can be diabetes, obesity, high blood pressure, heart problem or any major organ transplant. The contribution also increases if the face value is high. If a participant chooses to add supplementary cover (such as accidental death and indemnity, disability and annuities, among others), their contribution increases to reflect the wider scope of the cover. We will discuss supplementary covers in detail later in this chapter.

Investment Account

The rest of the participants' contribution is added to the investment account where it is pooled and invested in different avenues. Profit earned on investment is shared with clients. The pooled fund is divided into small units which are purchased for the clients when they pay their contribution. The value of units fluctuates depending on the performance of investments; therefore, each year, units are purchased and allocated to the individual investment accounts of the clients. On death or maturity or pre-mature withdrawal, cash value of the units is paid which is the multiple of total number of units and unit price on date of death, maturity or withdrawal date.

Money in this account is invested by the takaful company on the basis of mudarabah. Mudarabah is a type of partnership in which one or some partners provide capital, and one or some partners provide relevant skills to establish a partnership. Profit if earned is distributed according to the predetermined ratio by the partners. Capital-providing partner(s) is called rab ul maal, while the skill provider(s) is called mudarib. In case of loss, the capital provider bears the financial loss, while skill provider receives loss in terms of no return to his provided skills.[1]

Here, the participants' investment account is the rab ul maal and the takaful operator is the mudarib, as the operator is providing its investment expertise. The profit earned is divided between the participants' investment account and the takaful operator in a predetermined ratio.

If a participant dies, the beneficiary is paid a face value or cash value, whichever is greater. While at maturity stage, that is, if and when the duration of membership completes, the participant is only paid the cash value of the accumulated units.

Let's explain how this works with the help of a case study.

Case Study 6.2 Family Takaful Plan

Smith is 35 years old and works in a hospital as Head of Administration. He has two sons, John and Alan, and a wife, Karen. He wants to cover (although partially) the financial loss to his family if he dies. He also desires to make some savings and profits as well. Therefore, he takes out a family takaful cover as follows:

Face value: USD 100,000
Annual contribution: USD 12,000
Duration: 15 years
Participant's age at entry: 35 years
Beneficiary (nominee) = Karen

Based on Person A's age and the face value, an amount of USD 5000 is added to the participants' risk account, while the remaining USD 7000 is added to the participants' investment account.

After contributing for four years in the takaful fund, Smith dies.

(*continued*)

[1] K. Ullah & W. Al-Karaghouli, *Understanding Islamic financial services*. London: Kogan Page, 2017.

Case Study 6.2 (continued)

Karen, as a beneficiary, makes a claim to takaful operator which processes the claim and pays the beneficiary as follows:

Face value: USD 100,000

Cash value of the allocated units*: USD 40,000

Now face value is higher than the cash value of accumulated units; therefore, death claim equals to USD 100,000.

The break-up of the payable amount USD 100,000 is as follows: 60,000 is payable from risk account, while 40,000 is payable from the investment account.

*Each year, the takaful operator allocates units to participants' investment accounts. The number of units and the rate at which they are calculated depend on the investment performance of the underlying assets.

If the death of the participant occurs after 11 years of taking coverage:

Cash Value = USD 170,000

Face value = USD 1,000,000

Payable claim = 1,000,000

Break-up = 830,000 (from waqf) + 170,000 (from participant investment account or PIA)

830,000 + 170,000 = USD 1,000,000

Unit Pricing Methodology

As mentioned earlier, part of the participants' contribution goes into participant investment account (PIA), and units are purchased with it. Unit value of PIA changes with following cash inflows and outflows. Cash inflows occur when contribution is paid, and part of that contribution adds into PIA, and when profit is earned on the invested amount lying in PIA, it adds to PIA. Cash outflows occur when units are encashed and paid to the beneficiary or participant. Cash value of units is paid to the beneficiary if participant dies. Cash value of units is paid to the participant on early withdrawal or on maturity. Cash outflows also occur, when and if a loss occurs in investments. Based on these cash flows, unit price changes almost every day. Closing value of unit becomes opening value on the next day. All investments are made in Shariah-compliant investments and Shariah advisor ensures it. Takaful companies normally display the unit value on their websites which changes almost every day. An illustration showing the cash flows and opening and closing unit value is displayed in Exhibit 6.1.

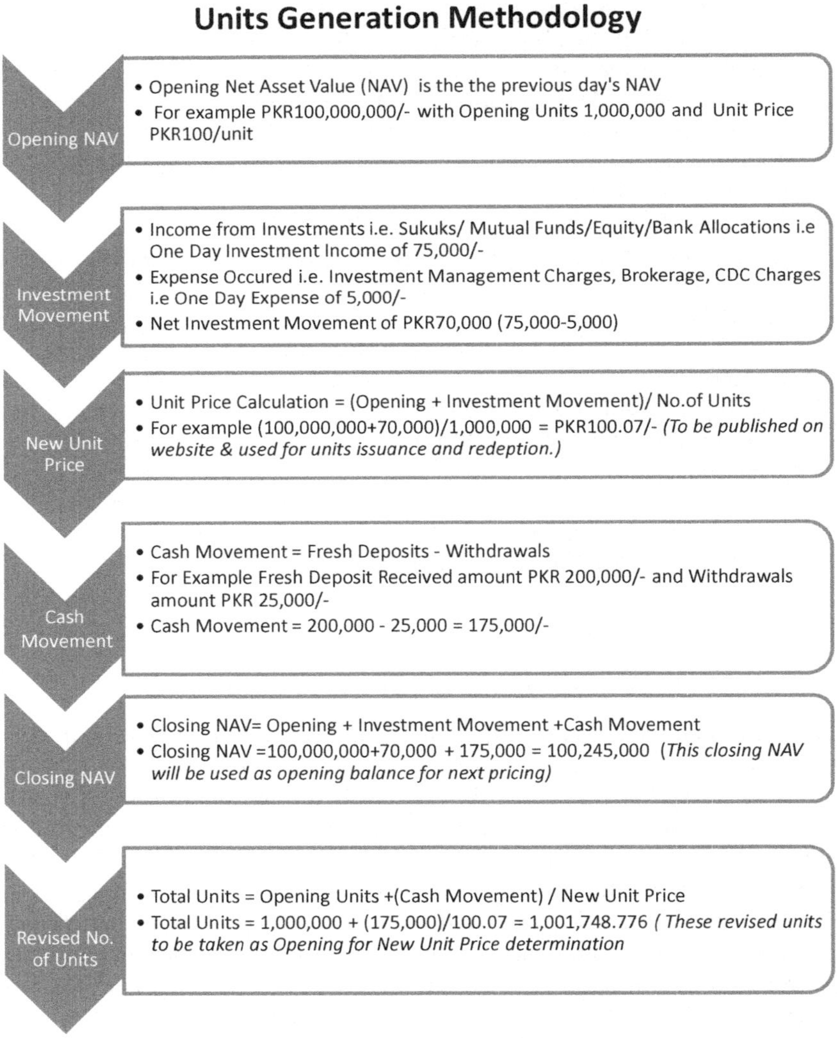

Exhibit 6.1 Unit pricing methodology

Generic Unit-Linked Family Takaful Coverages

Takaful companies offer different variations of unit-linked family takaful coverages. Companies develop different coverages for catering varying financial needs of a family. They give them catchy names like child protection, education and marriage plan, investment protection plan and life partner coverage. Let us discuss a few of them.

Family Protection Plan

This plan provides risk protection and savings for the participant. It provides lump sum payment if the participant dies and saving benefit if the plan matures. The term of the plan varies from 5 to 20 or 30 years. A whole life plan matures when the participant attains 85 years of age. It may also have a built-in annuity which provides an equal amount of payment on regular intervals if the participant dies.

Child Education Plan

Parents are always worried for the children's educational and upbringing expenses if the income-generating person (father) dies. A widow has to pay for different expenses like house rent, food and clothing and educational expenses of children. Therefore, married people are advised to take child education takaful plan, which has the provision of lump sum payment on death and a series of payments on regular intervals for child education expenses if participant dies.

Case Study 6.3 Child Education Plan
Mr Clark works as an accountant at a construction company. He has a small family: his wife Sarah, and six-year-old son Mark studying in class I at a nearby school. Sarah also works as an assistant in a hospital. Mr Clark earns sufficient money for their day-to-day expenses. He worries for his family if he dies. He wants Mark to acquire university education in a field of his choice. He knows that it won't happen if something wrong happens to him. Therefore, he decides taking a takaful plan having an annuity. Mark is appointed as beneficiary in it, and since he is not a major, Sarah, his mother, is appointed as guardian. Takaful plan he takes has the following details:

(*continued*)

Case Study 6.3 (continued)

Face value: USD 50,000
Annual contribution: USD 2000
Duration: 20 years
Participant's age at entry: 33 years
Coverage commencement date = 01.01.2013
Maturity date = 31.12.2033
Family income benefit (FIB) 20% for 20 years
Term takaful rider (TTR)
Beneficiary: Mark
Guardian: Mrs Sarah

After paying two annual contributions, Mr Clark dies due to a sudden heart attack on 31 December 2015.

Since Mark is a minor and has no contractual capacity, the payments will be made to Mrs Sarah, the guardian, till he becomes major. Therefore, Mrs Sarah makes a claim to takaful operator which processes the claim and pays as under:

Death claim calculation

Payment under basic contract

Face value: USD 50,000
Cash value of the allocated units*: USD 6000

Now face value is higher than the cash value of accumulated units; therefore, death claim under basic coverage equals to USD 50,000.

The break-up of the payable amount USD 50,000 is as follows: 44,000 is payable from risk account, while 6000 is payable from the investment account.

Riders:

Term takaful rider (TTR) = USD 50,000

FIB is payable for 18 years, that is, for the remaining period of coverage from date of death (maturity date minus date of death); 20% of 50,000 becomes 10,000, which is payable each year for 18 years.

Payable FIB for 18 years = 10000 × 18 = 180,000

Death claim payable

Face value	= 50,000
TTR	= 50,000
	100,000 lump sum payable on death
FIB	= 180,000
	282,000

USD 252,000 is payable to the widow. Only USD 4000 being cash value of units is paid from participant investment account, while the rest 248,000 is payable from the participant risk account.

Investment Protection Plan

This plan offers a safe and handsome return on the invested contribution and takaful coverage which ensures payment of the face value if the participant dies. It normally has a single large contribution which participates in investment of PIA. The term of the coverage varies from 05 to 15 years.

Retirement Income Plan

This plan provides takaful coverage in case of death, and retirement income if participant survives. Major portion of the contribution is paid into PIA where it is invested for earning profit. During this period, if a participant dies, the face value or cash value of units (whichever is higher) is paid. Maturity proceeds payable from PIA are paid in instalments (monthly or quarterly) to the participant for a specified number of years.

Life Partner Plan

In this plan, husband and wife cover in a single plan. If husband or wife dies, face value is paid from waqf fund to the surviving partner, and further contribution into PIA is made from waqf fund. The surviving partner appoints a new nominee, and in case of death, face value or cash value of units is paid. If surviving life partner survives till maturity, then cash value of units is paid.

Child Education and Marriage plan

In this plan, income-generating father or mother takes coverage and appoints their child as nominee. If the covered father or mother dies, takaful company starts paying the nominee on monthly or quarterly or half yearly or yearly basis, as agreed in the contract. This regular income is supposed to cover the educational expenses of children. On completion of coverage duration which normally happens when the nominee becomes major, a lump sum payment is paid to the nominee, considering it to be covering the marriage expenses.

Supplementary Benefit/Cover

A participant can increase the scope of their life cover by taking out supplementary cover. Supplementary cover can be attached to basic unit-linked or term takaful; supplementary covers are also called riders.

Contribution of riders paid by the participant goes only into participant risk account, and compensation occurs only if the participant dies. The compensation may also occur if the participant becomes disabled and disability income replacement rider is opted in coverage. Clients interested in higher compensation in case of death take riders with their basic coverage, while clients focusing on higher maturity value, that is, investment part of takaful, avoid riders and take higher face value, thus contributing more money into investment account.

We will look at the following examples of supplementary cover.

- Accidental death benefit (ADB)
- Accidental death and dismemberment (AD&D)
- Disability income replacement rider
- Family income benefit (FIB)
- Waiver of contribution
- Takaful-term rider
- Waiver of contribution
- Additional-term takaful

Accidental Death Benefit (ADB)

With this option, if the participant dies because of an accident, an additional face value is paid to the beneficiary on top of the basic face value. One or more ADB contracts can be attached to the cover.

Let's explain how ADB works with the help of a case study.

Case Study 6.4 Accidental Death Benefit (ADB)

Mr Shams works as an assistant in a law firm. He has three sons and a daughter, all studying, and a wife. He hardly covers the family expenses. He worries for the immediate financial family needs if he dies. Therefore, he takes out a family-term takaful cover along with supplementary contract ADB. The details are as follows:

Face value: USD 100,000

Supplementary cover: ADB

Mr Shams has an accident within a year and dies in hospital.

(*continued*)

Case Study 6.4 (continued)

The beneficiary makes a claim to the takaful operator, who compensates the beneficiary as follows:

Face value: USD 100,000

Additional face value due to accidental death: USD 100,000

Total paid to the beneficiary: USD 200,000

Accidental Death and Dismemberment (AD&D)

This option is similar to ADB in that if the participant dies because of an accident, an additional amount is paid to the beneficiary on top of the basic face value. However, if the participant survives the accident but has to have a limb amputated or suffers damage to their eyes, the participant receives compensation. This is paid to the participant in proportion to the injury they have received. For example, if a participant has to have one leg amputated after being in an accident, an amount equal to half of the face value due to AD&D cover will be paid to the participant, and the cover will continue.

Family Income Benefit (FIB)

To put it simply, FIB is an annuity. If a participant dies, a series of payments is made to the beneficiary at regular intervals.

Let's look at a case study of how FIB is calculated.

Case Study 6.5 Family Income Benefit (FIB)

Person B arranges family takaful cover with FIB as follows:

Face value: USD 100,000

Duration of cover: 20 years

FIB: 10% of the face value for the remaining term of the cover.

After paying contribution for five years, Person B dies.

Person B's beneficiary makes a claim to the takaful operator. The compensation made to the beneficiary will be as follows:

(*continued*)

Case Study 6.5 (continued)

Face value: USD 100,000

FIB at 10% of the face value for the remaining term of the cover: USD 10,000 a year for 15 years = 150,000

So, Person B's beneficiary receives a lump sum of USD 100,000, followed by 15 annual payments of USD 10,000.

Disability Income Replacement Rider

This rider provides income replacement if a person becomes disabled. The disability can be temporary or permanent, and partial or total. Moreover, the disability can be natural or accidental. If the wrist of a driver fractures in an accident taking six months for recovery and is unable to drive for six months, he is thus completely off the work. Recovery period is six months, so the disability is temporary. Instead of fracture, if it was wrist amputation, then it could be permanent disability. Moreover, the driver is completely off the work for six months, therefore disability is total. If he can join another profession within six months, then the disability will be partial in nature. Income replacement is maximum in total disability, while partly in case of partial disability.

Case Study 6.6 Disability Income Replacement

Mr Ady, a motor mechanic supervisor, met with an accident while travelling on a highway. With other minor injuries, his right arm also fractured. Doctors advised him for complete bed rest for three months while the arm would take six months to heal.

The disability is therefore temporary, total for three months and partial for the remaining three months as he could supervise his staff. If he is covered against the risk of financial loss due to disability, then the company would be compensating him for total disability for three months and partial for the next three months.

Waiver of Contribution

This rider waives off the remaining contributions of the coverage if the participant becomes disabled due to accident or disease. Waqf fund pays contribution for buying units in PIA till death or maturity. So, units in the participant investment account increase without paying contribution. Meanwhile, if the participant dies, the beneficiary is compensated as the participant was paying the contribution himself during the disability period.

Case Study 6.7 Family Takaful with Waiver of Contribution Rider
Mr Shah arranges family takaful cover with FIB as follows:

Face value: USD 20,000
Duration of cover: 15 years
Entry age = 25 years
Profession = crane operator
Riders:
FIB: 10% of the face value for the remaining term of the cover
Accidental death benefit (ADB)
Waiver of contribution
Annual contribution = USD 900

After paying contribution for five years, Person B dies.

Person B's beneficiary makes a claim to the takaful operator. The compensation made to the beneficiary will be as follows:

Face value: USD 100,000

FIB at 10% of the face value for the remaining term of the cover: USD 10,000 a year for 15 years = 150,000

So, Person B's beneficiary receives a lump sum of USD 100,000, followed by 15 annual payments of USD 10,000.

Additional-Term Takaful

An additional face value is paid to the beneficiary if the participant dies. It will be paid whether participant dies naturally or due to an accident.

Case Study 6.8 Life Partner Unit-Linked Family Takaful with Riders
Mr and Mrs Ali, aged 35 and 30 years, respectively, take out unit-linked family takaful in which husband and wife are covered with riders as follows:

Face value: USD 40,000
Annual contribution: USD 4000
Duration: 20 years

(*continued*)

Case Study 6.8 (continued)

Participant's age at entry: 30 years

Coverage commencement date = 01.01.2012

Maturity date = 31.12.2032

FIB 20% for 20 years

Accidental death benefit

Term takaful rider (TTR)

Beneficiary: surviving life partner

After paying four annual contributions, Mr Ali dies in a road traffic accident on 30 June 2015.

Mrs Ali as beneficiary makes a claim to the takaful operator. The takaful operator processes the claim and pays the beneficiary as follows:

Death claim calculation

Face value: USD 40,000

Cash value of the allocated units*: USD 5000

Now face value is higher than the cash value of accumulated units; therefore, death claim under basic coverage equals to USD 40,000

The break-up of the payable amount USD 40,000 = 35,000 is payable from risk account, while 5000 is payable from the investment account.

Death is due to an accident, therefore additional face value is payable from the risk account.

Under term takaful, an additional face value is payable from the risk account. FIB is payable for 16 years and 06 months, that is, for the remaining period of coverage from date of death (maturity date minus date of death), 20% of 40,000 becomes 8000, which is payable each year for 16 years and six months. For six months, 4000 is payable.

Payable FIB for 16 years = 8000 × 16 = 128,000

For six-month, payable FIB = 4000

Total payable FIB = 132000

Death claim payable

Face value = 40,000

ADB = 40,000

(*continued*)

Case Study 6.8 (continued)

TTR = 40,000
FIB = 132,000
252,000

USD 252,000 is payable to the widow. Only USD 4000 being cash value of units is paid from participant investment account, while the rest 248,000 is payable from the participant risk account.

Mrs Ali will appoint another beneficiary, and if she also dies, the beneficiary will be compensated in similar way.

Indexation Clause

Unit-linked takaful are long-term contracts, and inflation reduces the benefits. For instance, a client takes coverage for 20 years having a face value USD 50,000. Participant survives and doesn't die in 20 years. The maturity proceeds can be somewhere USD 100,000. This amount seems attractive now, but after 20 years, it may not be that much handsome. Therefore, to keep the face value relevant in relation to inflation, indexation clause can be opted which can increase the face value increase annually by 5%, 10%, 15% and 20% annually. There is also a proportionate increase in contribution.

Top-Up Contribution

In unit-linked takaful plan, a participant can buy more units in the investment account if in additional amount is paid along with regular contribution. This additional amount is called top-up contribution and is like an extra topping of, say, mushrooms and chicken on pizzas.

Group Term Family Takaful

Term family takaful provides cover for a relatively short period, such as one year. It provides death benefit only. Therefore, if someone takes out term-life cover for one year and survives, unlike unit-linked takaful, they will not receive any payment when the cover ends.

Usually, term family cover is usually taken out as a group, but an individual can also take it. For example, employers may provide group family cover for their employees so that if an employee dies in service, the takaful operator will pay a death claim to the employee's beneficiary. Individuals also take out term family cover, but this is rare. All contribution of the participants goes into the risk account, so there is no maturity value but only death benefit. Not all but some supplementary contracts/riders can also be attached with term life family takaful like accidental death benefit, accidental death and dismemberment benefit and disability rider.

Credit Family Cover

Sometimes, lending institutions require the borrower to take out term family takaful with face value equal to the outstanding amount of the loan. Face value reduces as the outstanding amount also decreases due to repayments. Banks also take this cover in credit cards. Microfinance institutions also use this cover when they provide microcredit facility to their borrowers. Individuals can also take this cover when they borrow money from someone covering the outstanding amount. If the borrower dies before repaying the loan, the death claim is paid to the lending institution up to the amount outstanding.

Case Study 6.9 Credit Family Takaful Cover
Mr Eden borrowed USD 2000 for one year from United Microfinance Institution which provides interest-free loan to low-income people. Eden needed money for the expansion of his small grocery business. United also takes credit cover for their borrowers from a family takaful company for the outstanding loan. So if any borrower dies without repaying the loan, takaful company pays the balance loan and deceased family is not required to repay the loan to United. In this way, recovery of loans by United improves, and the deceased family is also not required to pay the outstanding loan.

Mr Eden dies after repaying USD 1000. United lodges a claim with takaful company, and after processing, USD 1000 is paid to United Microfinance Institution.

Case Study 6.10 Group Term Family Takaful

Excellent University takes out term family takaful coverage for all of its staff with following coverage details:

Face value = USD 50,000

Accidental death benefit

One of its employees dies in road traffic accident within a year. University lodges a claim with company, which pays the claim after processing to the deceased family. Details are as under:

Death claim payable

Face value	= USD 50,000
ADB	= USD 50,000
	100,000

Supplementary Takaful Benefits

The following supplementary benefits can be attached to a basic plan, and their benefits mentioned in the following section are subject to the terms and conditions as defined in the participant membership document (PMD).

Critical Illness

The cost of healthcare and convalescence for long-standing disease is increasing day by day. The financial impact of such diseases can increase, with the customer being compelled to quit his vocation; this supplemental benefit covers 22 major illnesses including, but not limited to, cancer, major heart attack, major organ transplant and even accidental amputation of two limbs. The cover provides a lump sum pay-out in case an individual undergoes any such critical illness.

Takaful Accidental Death and Dismemberment

This supplementary benefit is to cover disability and death due to accident, providing extra payments to participants or their beneficiaries who suffer fatal accidents, dismemberments or accidental, total or permanent disability.

Takaful Accidental Death Benefit

This supplementary benefit provides additional coverage in case of death of participant caused by an accident.

Takaful Family Income Benefit

This supplementary benefit provides a mutually agreed upon monthly income to the beneficiary if the participant dies. The payment continues till maturity of the specified period.

Takaful Waiver of Contribution

Under this coverage, all future regular contributions waive off if the participant is disabled permanently due to an accident or disease. The waqf fund will pay the contribution to the investment account on behalf of the participant. The coverage under the basic plan will continue as usual.

Takaful Hospital Daily Allowance

In an event of a participant's hospitalisation for more than two consecutive days, a predefined daily allowance for coverage of medical expenses or for loss of income during the period of hospitalisation will be provided.

Chapter Summary

This chapter has focused on the different services that family takaful companies offer. These services can be divided into:

- Unit-linked family takaful, which pays compensation to beneficiaries if a participant dies or becomes disabled and also has a saving element if a participant survives the coverage duration.
- Family-term takaful, which provides only death benefit.

Basic cover can be expanded by adding appropriate supplementary clauses to the contract. In family takaful, supplementary clauses, such as AD&D or an annuity, can be added to the basic contract.

CHAPTER 7

General Takaful

Abstract This chapter has focused on the different services that a general takaful company offers. These services can be divided into motor takaful, fire takaful and engineering takaful. In motor takaful, the waqf fund pays compensation to the participant in case of accidental damage, both partial and total, theft and third-party liability. Fire takaful provides compensation to the participant if their property including building, machinery and physical stock is damaged due to fire, earthquake and atmospheric disturbance (flood, hurricane, snow effect, etc.). Engineering takaful provides compensation to the participant if damage occurs to industrial boilers and construction machinery like bulldozers and cranes.

Keywords Engineering takaful • Fire takaful • General takaful • Motor takaful

After reading this chapter, you should understand:

- Types of general takaful services: motor, fire, marine, engineering and miscellaneous
- Supplementary benefits (riders) offered in family and general takaful
- The concepts of under-coverage and over-coverage

A. Malik, K. Ullah, *Introduction to Takaful*,
https://doi.org/10.1007/978-981-32-9016-7_7

Introduction

Takaful cover other than family takaful falls under the category of general takaful. This includes cover for property (such as vehicles, aeroplanes, buildings, machinery, physical stock and cash) against risks (such as fire, earthquakes, riots and strikes, accidents, terrorism, floods, burglary and theft).

The most important features of general takaful cover are as follows:

- *The contracts are usually short term* (one year or less). Participants' contributions may vary from year to year. For example, a person does not have to contribute as much for motor takaful cover if they have not had an accident before. However, if that person does have an accident, they will have to make a higher contribution in the following year: the fact that they have an accident in their driving history means that they bring more risk to the fund.
- *All general takaful cover is indemnity cover.* As discussed in Chap. 2, non-life cover is indemnity cover because it aims to return the person to the financial circumstances they were in before the loss occurred. Family takaful cover is different: because no financial value can be placed on human life, the compensation paid to the beneficiary is not intended to return them to the same financial circumstances they were in before the death. Rather, it aims to ease the financial burden placed on the beneficiary as a result of the participant's death.
- *Paying a claim may or may not end a contract.* In family takaful, if a participant dies, a claim is paid to the beneficiary and the cover ends. This is not the case in general takaful. For example, in motor takaful, if a car is partly damaged in an accident, it will be repaired, compensation for partial loss will be paid to the participant and the cover will continue until the term of the agreement ends.
- *The risk covered does not necessarily increase over time.* In family takaful, the risk of death increases with the passage of time, as the mortality rate increases with age. However, the risk of loss associated with property (e.g., a car) does not usually increase with each passing year.

The following types of general takaful are available.

- Motor
- Fire
- Engineering
- Marine
- Miscellaneous accidents

These are discussed in more detail in the rest of this section.

Motor Takaful

When a person drives a vehicle on the road, that person faces the risk of having an accident in which the vehicle could be damaged or destroyed. It could also be stolen, or the driver could injure someone or damage other people's property (such as another car or a shop window). To manage the financial consequences of these events, car owners can become participants of a takaful fund by making a contribution in accordance with their level of risk.

Types of Cover

Three types of cover are available:

- Third-party liability
- Third party, fire and theft
- Comprehensive

Third-Party Liability

This type of cover protects participants against claims if, when using their vehicle, they:

- Injure or kill another person (known as the third party)
- Damage another person's (third party's) property

Third Party, Fire and Theft

This type of cover provides protection against claims for:

- Injuring or killing another person (third party)
- Damaging a third party's property
- A participant's own vehicle being accidentally damaged by fire or stolen

Comprehensive Cover

This type of cover provides the highest level of protection. In addition to the risks covered by third party, fire and theft protection, it covers loss or damage to a participant's own vehicle in an accident, even if the accident is their fault.

Motor takaful proposal form is displayed at Exhibit 7.1 for further understanding.

Calculating Participant Contributions

Takaful operators usually base the contribution a participant should contribute on a percentage of the value of the car or other vehicle, along with other factors. We will explain the other factors that are taken into account later in this chapter and in Chap. 9.

Case Study 7.1 Calculating Contributions for Motor Takaful

Person A contacts a takaful operator to arrange motor takaful for a car worth USD 20,000. The takaful operator calculates the basic contribution rate using a rate of 3.5% of the value of the vehicle.

Value of the car (sum assured): USD 20,000

Contribution rate: 3.5% of sum assured = USD 700.

Under-coverage and Over-coverage

If a person covers their vehicle for a sum that is lower than its market value, they will be deemed as self-insured for the difference. That is, if the vehicle is stolen or damaged, the takaful operator will pay a proportion of the claim that is equal to the proportion of the market value covered.

If a person covers their vehicle for a sum that is higher than its market value, the maximum compensation the takaful operator will pay is the market value of the vehicle. This is because participants cannot make a profit from a motor takaful claim.

Let us look at how this works with the help of a case study.

GENERAL TAKAFUL

Pak-Qatar General Takaful Limited

Suite # 402-404
Business Arcade
Block 6, Sharea Faisal
P.E.C.H.S,
Karachi

Contact Details:
Phone (92 21) 34380357-61
Fax No. (92 21) 34386453
Email: info@pakqatar.com.pk
Web: www.pakqatar.com.pk

MOTOR VEHICLE TAKAFUL PROPOSAL FORM

PARTICULARS OF PROPOSER

NAME OF OWNER/BANK/CAR IJARAH ____ **Metrotex Industries**

C.N.I.C. NO OF THE USER ____

ADDRESS: ____ **F- 61 / C S.I.T.E, KARACHI.**

____ Karachi

TEL NO. (OFF/MOB): ____ **0345-9226909** (RES) ____ (FAX) ____

Would you like to be on our SMS mailing list? ☐ Yes ☐ No

BUSINESS OR PROFESSION: ____

REFERENCE THROUGH: ____

VEHICLE TYPE: ☐ PRIVATE CAR ■ MOTOR CYCLE ☐ COMMERCIAL VEHICLE

COVERAGE REQUIRED ■ COMPREHENSIVE ☐ THIRD PARTY ☐ ACT ONLY

PARTICULARS OF THE VEHICLE

REGISTRATION NO: ____ **KFH-3536** C.C.: ____ **70**

MAKE: ____**HONDA**____ MODEL: ____ **2011** COLOUR: **BLACK**

ENGINE NO. ____**2967393**____ CHASSIS NO. ____ **AJ860773**

MILEAGE: ____**21210KMS**____ VALUE TO BE COVERED Rs. ____ **55,000**

PERIOD OF INSURANCE FROM ____ TO ____

PARKING CONDITIONS ☐ GARAGE ☐ WITHIN COMPOUND ☐ OPEN SPACE

ACCESSORIES FITTED IN THE VEHICLE

ACCESSORIES	PLEASE TICK ( )		IF OTHER THAN FACTORY FITTED		
	FACTORY FITTED	OTHERS	MAKE	MODEL	VALUE (RS)
RADIO/CASSETTE PLAYER					
CD/ DVD PLAYER					
AIR CONDITIONER					
C.N.G. KIT					
ALLOY RIMS					
ANY OTHER ITEMS					

ATTACHED COPIES OF:
(*) Registration Book/Transfer Slip
(*) C.N.I.C. of the Participant
( ) Last Renewal Notice (if entitled to NCD)
( ) Tracker Installation Certificate/Invoice (if installed with vehicle)
( ) Any Other (Please specify) ____

Exhibit 7.1 Motor takaful proposal form

PREVIOUS HISTORY OF CLAIMS, IF ANY

Sr. No.	Date of Loss	Company Name	Amount Claimed / Paid			
1						
2						
3						
4						
5						

DECLARATION

1 I/We hereby confirm that the details contained in this proposal form are true and correct to the best of my/our knowledge and belief and I/We have not concealed, misrepresented or misstated any material fact. I/We further undertake to inform the company of any material alterations to these facts occuring during the currency of this Policy.

2 I/We agree that the statements and declaration contained in this proposal form shall be the basis of my/our beneficiar y status in the Takaful Fund and deemed to be incorporated in the Policy.

3 I/We hereby undertake to contribute the agreed amount to the Takaful Fund maintained and operated by the company.

4 I/We understand that as per the rules of Takaful Fund, by doing so I shall stand entitled to the membership of the Takaful Fund and being one of its beneficiaries subject to the rules and regulations of the Fund.

5 As a prospective beneficiary of the Fund, I/We offer my/our property, as specifically described in the attached schedule, for the indemnity cover provided by the Fund to its beneficiaries.

6 I/We hereby request to be issued with a confirmation to acknowledge my membership and my consequentia l rights as a beneficiary of the Fund.

Signed at: ____________________ Signature of the Participants: ________________

Dated ☐☐☐☐☐☐☐☐ Name of Signatory: ________________

(FOR OFFICE USE ONLY)

MOTOR VEHICLE INSPECTION REPORT

1 Particulars of the vehicle declared by proposer are

☐ Correct ☐ If not (Please specify the reason with details) ____________________

____

2 Condition of the vehicle at the time of inspection: ____________________

Details of existing damages, if any ____________________

____

Condition of colour: ☐ Good ☐ Fair ☐ Faded

3 Bonus/loading position: (Please attach copy of renewal notice) ____________________

____

4 Tracker Installed: ☐ Yes (attach copy of tracker certificate/invoice) ☐ No.

5 Details of accessories mentioned by proposer are

☐ Cover ☐ If not (Please specify the reason with details) ____________________

____

Signature( )
Name of authorised Officer ____________________

Dated ☐☐☐☐☐☐☐☐

Signature of proposer or on behalf of proposer
Name of Signatory: ____________________

Dated ☐☐☐☐☐☐☐☐

The liability of the Company does not commence until the Proposal has been accepted and the contribution paid. Only official receipt issued from the Company on printed form is binding on the Company

Exhibit 7.1 (continued)

Case Study 7.2 Under-Coverage and Over-Coverage

Under-coverage

Mr Shah arranges takaful cover for his car as follows:

Market value of car: USD 50,000

Sum assured: USD 25,000.

In this case, Shah has covered 50% of the value of the car. Therefore, if any claim arises, the takaful operator will pay 50% of the claim, but Shah will have to bear the remaining 50%. If an accident occurs and the value of the loss is USD 20,000, the takaful operator will pay USD 10,000, and the client will have to pay USD 10,000.

Over-coverage

Mr Jeffry arranges takaful cover for his car as follows:

Market value of car: USD 40,000

Sum assured: USD 50,000.

In this case, Jeffry has covered the car for a sum assured that is more than the car's market value. If the car is stolen or destroyed beyond repair, the company will pay no more than USD 40,000, as according to the motor coverage document, in case of theft or total loss, company will pay the sum covered or the market value, whichever is less.

Excess Loss

The excess is also known as a deductible. This is the amount of loss that the participant has to bear before the takaful operator will pay the balance of the claim. Let us suppose a person has comprehensive cover with an excess of USD 500. If a loss of USD 20,000 occurs, the takaful operator will pay USD 19,500, and the participant will have to bear the excess of USD 500.

If there is an excess, it is not possible to claim for losses that are lower than the excess. So, in the earlier example, the participant cannot claim for losses up to USD 500. However, having an excess in place may reduce the contribution rate (e.g., from 3.5% to 3.3%). It has a benefit both for the participant and for the company. The participant will not claim for small loses, thus avoiding the fatigue and taking a discount in the contribution. The company will reduce its risk although by a small amount but will be free from the administrative hustle it takes while settling a claim.

Applying the Principle of Indemnity in Motor Takaful Claims

Based on the principle of indemnity, takaful operators will compensate participants for their loss by returning them to the financial position they were in immediately before the loss.

As participants are compensated only for the loss they have suffered, they cannot profit from a motor takaful claim. Therefore, if a vehicle is more than six months old, depreciation will apply. The depreciation rate for each year is set by considering the useful life of the vehicle to be covered. For instance, in some markets, useful life of a vehicle is considered to be 10 years. So, each year, its value is depreciated by 10%.

The period for applying depreciation is calculated with the difference between the date when loss occurs and the date when the vehicle was manufactured. If a vehicle is partly damaged and it is two years old, the takaful company bears 80% of the cost of the new parts while the participant bears 20% of the cost, as the participant has already consumed 20% life of that particular part.

Therefore, betterment occurs when a vehicle that is damaged in an accident is repaired by replacing an old part with a new one. In line with the principle of indemnity, the participant has to pay the difference in costs, because having the new part puts them in a better financial position after the accident than they were in before it happened.

Let's look at a case study of how depreciation is applied.

Case Study 7.3 Depreciation

A vehicle covered by a motor takaful scheme met with an accident in 2018. The loss is estimated as follows.

Total claim: USD 10,000
Labour charge: USD 3000
Cost of new parts: USD 7000
Year of manufacture of the vehicle: 2014 (it is four years old)

Depreciation is applied to the cost of new parts at a rate of 10% for each year of the age of the car. Therefore, in this case, depreciation is applied to the cost of new parts (USD 7000) at a rate of 40%. This comes to USD 2800.

The participant must pay USD 2800 towards the cost of the new parts, while the takaful operator will pay the other USD 4200 and the labour charge (USD 3000). Therefore, the total compensation paid to the participant is USD 7200.

Setting the Contribution in Motor Takaful

Companies decide what the contribution will be by looking at the overall cost of reported or expected claims and other expenses. The following case study illustrates how the contribution is calculated.

Case Study 7.4 Calculating the Contribution

A takaful operator is covering 10,000 vehicles, each for a sum assured of USD 30,000. Suppose the operator receives 500 claims.

Total amount claimed: USD 7500,000 (A)

Total number of claims payable: 500 (B)

Average claim amount: (A ÷ B) = 7500,000/500 = USD 15,000 (C)

Number of people covered: 10,000 (D)

Premium to be charged for every vehicle: (A ÷ D) = 7500, 000/10,000 = USD 750.

Please note: We have ignored the administrative expense and profit margin in this case study for keeping it simple.

A complete Commercial Motor takaful policy is displayed at Exhibit 7.2 for knowing more details.

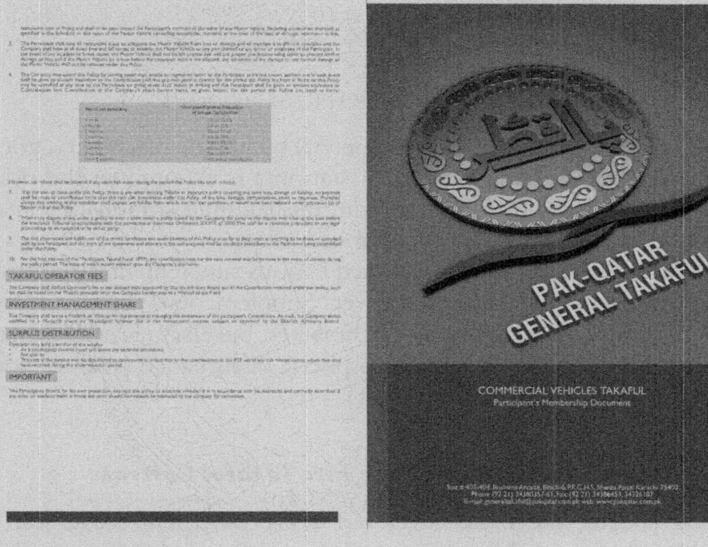

Exhibit 7.2 Commercial Motor takaful Policy

(continued)

Case Study 7.4 (continued)

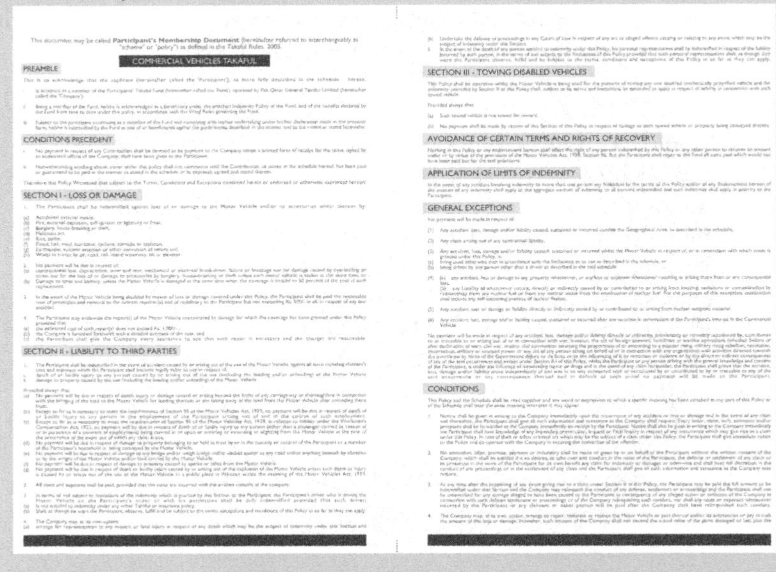
This document may be called **Participant's Membership Document** (hereinafter referred to interchangeably as "scheme" or "policy") as defined in the Takaful Rules 2005.

COMMERCIAL VEHICLES TAKAFUL

PREAMBLE

CONDITIONS PRECEDENT

SECTION I - LOSS OR DAMAGE

SECTION II - LIABILITY TO THIRD PARTIES

SECTION III - TOWING DISABLED VEHICLES

AVOIDANCE OF CERTAIN TERMS AND RIGHTS OF RECOVERY

APPLICATION OF LIMITS OF INDEMNITY

GENERAL EXCEPTIONS

CONDITIONS

Exhibit 7.2 (continued)

Fire Takaful

Property (such as residential and commercial buildings, machinery, goods, electronics, electrical items and petrol stations) is exposed to the risk of fire. Fire can be caused by a short circuit, mishandling combustible material and other accidents. It can result in heavy losses.

Over time, companies have developed various supplementary contracts to expand the scope of basic fire cover. Supplementary cover provides compensation for losses caused by earthquakes, burglary, aircraft damage, explosions, riots and strikes, and atmospheric disturbance (such as flooding, cyclones, heavy snow and drought).

Clauses that Increase Basic Fire Takaful Coverage

In general takaful, the basic cover is for fire only. This cover can be extended by adding supplementary cover for risks related to fire, which are known as allied perils. Peril basically means exposure to a hazard or danger.

Such risks can be covered by adding supplementary clauses to the basic fire cover. For example, let's suppose that some machinery in a factory needs to be covered against the risk of damage from flood, burglary, and riots and strikes in addition to the risk of damage from fire. First, the machinery has to be covered against the risk of fire, which is the basic form of cover that has to be arranged. Cover against the risk of loss caused by flood, burglary, and riots and strikes (damage by employees or others) is added by making additional contributions for this supplementary cover.

The different types of supplementary clauses to fire takaful cover are explained in the following section. All of these clauses cover only property that is already covered by basic fire takaful.

Earthquake, Fire and Shock

This clause covers loss caused by fire, earthquakes or shock. During an earthquake, the structure of a building may remain intact, but the concealed electrical wiring may be damaged by shock. This may result in a short circuit, which can lead to fire and damage the building and the belongings inside. This type of fire is not covered by ordinary fire takaful, because the proximate (root) cause of the fire is not the short-circuiting itself but the shocks from an earthquake. As such, the losses will be covered only if the supplementary earthquake, fire and shock cover has been added to the basic fire cover.

Atmospheric Disturbance

An atmospheric disturbance clause covers loss or damage to property caused by the following weather conditions.

- Hail (pellets of frozen rain, which can cause damage on impact), snow, wind, hurricanes (storms with a very strong wind), cyclones (a system of strong winds rotating inwards to an area of low pressure from an area of high pressure) and tornados
- Flood, which includes:
  - Natural or man-made watercourses (such as rivers, canals or dams) overflowing or flowing outside their normal channels
  - Water flowing or building up on the ground, except when the water has come from a water supply main, tap, pipe or valve

Electrical Clauses A and B

This type of electrical clause covers loss or damage to electrical appliances and installations caused by fire that starts because of overrunning, excessive pressure, short-circuiting, arcing, self-heating or leakage of electricity, from whatever cause (including lightning). Electrical clause A does not cover damage to the appliance that caused the fire but does cover fire damage to other appliances. Electrical clause B covers the damage to other appliances in addition to the appliance that caused the fire.

Impact Damage

An impact damage clause covers loss or damage caused by something hitting the property. It includes impact from vehicles, horses or cattle that do not belong to and are not in the control of the participant or the participant's employees. An example of when this supplementary cover would apply is a vehicle colliding with a petrol station and causing damage.

Malicious Damage

A malicious damage clause covers loss or damage that someone causes deliberately (whether or not they do this during a riot or other public disturbance).

Aircraft Damage

An aircraft damage clause covers loss that is directly caused by an aircraft and other aerial devices or articles, such as a fuel tank dropping from a plane. Pilots are usually advised to get rid of their fuel tanks in certain emergencies. These may fall on homes, cars or buildings, causing damage.

Explosions

An explosion clause covers any loss or damage caused by a fire resulting from an explosion or otherwise directly caused by the explosion. For example, if a lorry's fuel tank explodes while the driver is filling it at a petrol station, the losses will be covered if the petrol station has supplementary explosion cover. This cover does not include loss or damage to boilers, economisers or other machinery or equipment in which pressure is used, and it does not cover their contents.

Under an explosion clause, the takaful operator does not cover loss or damage caused by (directly or indirectly) acts of terrorism committed by individuals or groups acting on behalf of or in connection with any organisation. In this context, terrorism means using violence for political purposes, which includes causing fear among the public.

If the participant and the takaful operator disagree about whether a loss is covered or not, the participant is responsible for proving that the loss is covered.

Riot and Strike Damage
Oxford dictionary defines 'Riot' as 'a violent disturbance of the peace by a crowd' and 'Strike' with reference to employees, as a refusal to work organised by a body of employees 'as a form of protest, typically in an attempt to gain a concession or concessions from their employer'.

Losses due to riots may occur in an area when an angry mob attacks a property and causes damages to it. Takaful company will compensate the loss only if the loss due to riots is covered in the coverage.

Burglary
It covers the losses that occur due to unlawful entry of burglars in a covered premise (Insuranceopedia). Companies provide compensation only if there is no insider's help with the burglary and the entry into the premises is forcible and foreseeable, for instance, burglars have broken the lock, door, deactivated alarm system or broken the wall.

Let's look at some case studies of underwriting for fire takaful.

Case Study 7.5 Fire Takaful
Mr Ali is running a pharmaceutical distribution firm covering a large area. He keeps a physical stock of medicine of around one million in godown which is located in a place which is exposed to floods, earthquake, riots and strikes. Therefore, he takes takaful coverage against the risk of fire and given the allied perils. The takaful operator calculates annual contribution as follows.

Required cover	*Rate (USD Per 100 of sum covered)*	*Contribution (based on sum assured of USD 01 million)*
Fire and lightning	0.005%	00.005 × USD 1,000,000 = USD 5000
Earthquake, fire and shock	0.06%	0.006 × USD 1,000,000 = USD 6000
Atmospheric disturbance	0.01%	0.001 × USD 1,000,000 = USD 1000
Total annual contribution		USD 12,000

A complete fire takaful policy is displayed at Exhibit 7.3.

(*continued*)

Case Study 7.5 (continued)

TAKAFUL OPERATOR FEES

INVESTMENT MANAGEMENT SHARE

SURPLUS DISTRIBUTION

IMPORTANT

PAK-QATAR GENERAL TAKAFUL

FIRE TAKAFUL POLICY

Participant's Membership Document

This document may be called **Participant's Membership Document** (hereinafter referred to interchangeably as "scheme" or "policy") as defined in the Takaful Rules, 2005.

FIRE TAKAFUL POLICY

PREAMBLE

CONDITIONS PRECEDENT

CONDITIONS

Exhibit 7.3 Fire takaful policy

Engineering Takaful

This type of takaful is often referred to as plant and machinery. There are two main types of engineering takaful, which are explained in the following section.

Boiler and Pressure Takaful

Factories that have boilers need to take great care when handling the steam pressure. High pressure builds up in these boilers in order to heat various items to very high temperatures—sometimes over 1000 degrees centigrade. Occasionally, the steam pressure built up in the boiler for heating purposes gets out of control and the boiler explodes, causing large amounts of damage. These explosions are not covered by basic fire takaful. Instead, customised cover has to be arranged for boilers. This is usually called pressure vessel cover.

Electrical/Mechanical Takaful

There is always a risk that electrical and mechanical equipment will break down. These breakdowns are not covered by basic or supplementary fire takaful, so separate, specialised cover has to be arranged.

For example, if an air conditioner stops working because of an internal fault, the cost of repairing or replacing the faulty parts will be covered only if electrical items cover has been arranged.

Marine Takaful

Marine takaful provides cover for various risks when goods are transported from one place to another by sea, air, rail or road. Marine takaful can cover the goods and the carrier (ship, aeroplane and so on). It is called marine takaful because it was first provided when merchants had to use ships to transport goods overseas.

Takaful operators provide three main types of marine cover: A, B and C.

- Type A offers the maximum cover.
- Type B provides less cover than type A but more than type C.
- Type C provides the least cover.

Takaful for Miscellaneous Items

Cash Takaful

Businesses dealing in cash (such as banks, currency exchanges, distribution firms and supermarkets) need cover for the risk of robbery. Businesses keep cash in a counter or in a safe, and they may also have to transport it. Usually, businesses keep a small amount of cash in the counter for small deals, while the rest of the cash is kept in a safe and then moved to a bank.

Cash at Counter

Businesses need cash in the counter for day-to-day transactions. However, there is a risk that somebody could come in and use force and violence to steal this cash. Cash takaful provides cover for this risk. The sum assured is usually lower than the sum assured for cash kept in a safe or in transit.

Cash at Safe

Cash takaful can also cover cash kept in a safe (e.g., in a shop, distribution firm, currency exchange, mobile franchise or bank)

Cash in Transit

When distributing products, such as medicine or food items, companies deliver them in exchange for cash, which they bring back to the office. Such cash is then moved to the bank. Takaful operators cover the cash while it is being transported: this is called cash in transit cover.

Personal Accident

Personal accident takaful covers only accidental death. Death due to natural causes, such as a heart attack, is not covered. There is always a set term, and unlike family takaful, there is no savings element.

Worker Compensation Cover

This type of takaful provides cover to employees who are injured at work. It includes compensation for employees' medical and rehabilitation costs and their lost wages. Every country has its own laws for ensuring compensation to workers. In Pakistan, under the Workmen's Compensation Act 1923, employers must compensate their employees if they are injured at work. Takaful companies have arranged policies that provide the minimum compensation by law. The employer must give the takaful operator details about its employees in order for the cover to be provided.

Chapter Summary

This chapter has focused on the different services that a general takaful company offers. These services can be divided into:

- Motor takaful, which pays compensation to the participant in case of accidental damage, both partial and total, theft and third-party liability.
- Fire takaful, which provides compensation to the participant if their property including building, machinery and physical stock is damaged due to fire, earthquake, atmospheric disturbance (flood, hurricane, snow effect, etc.).
- Engineering takaful which provides compensation to the participant if damage occurs to industrial boilers and construction machinery like bulldozers and cranes.

CHAPTER 8

Re-takaful

Abstract For better risk mitigation, takaful operators often share their risks with re-takaful companies. Re-takaful companies also use wakalah and mudarabah models for their operations. Takaful companies arrange re-takaful for increasing their underwriting and claim-paying capacities. There are two broad types of re-takaful agreements, namely, facultative and treaty re-takaful, which have further subtypes including proportional and non-proportional.

Keywords Facultative Re-takaful • Risk sharing • Re-Takaful • Treaty Re-Takaful

After reading this chapter, you should understand:

- The concept and mechanism of re-takaful
- History, types and motives of re-takaful
- The issues and challenges being faced by re-takaful companies

Takaful companies are risk-taking entities. Sometimes, they need to cover large risks, for instance, multimillion-dollar manufacturing units, buildings, bridges, power stations, ships and aeroplanes. For covering such

A. Malik, K. Ullah, *Introduction to Takaful*,
https://doi.org/10.1007/978-981-32-9016-7_8

risks, the companies need to have large claim funds sufficient enough to cover the losses. For covering such assets, they always take several measures for managing these risks. A takaful and an insurance company always avoid providing 100% insurance coverage in such high-value items and projects, as any complete loss in these items can result in big cash outflow. But they cannot afford to lose the contribution coming from such coverages. So, they share some of their risk with other companies specialised in such coverages. This process of sharing risk with other specialised companies is called re-takaful. We may call it takaful for takaful companies.

History shows large losses which could result in insolvencies of insurance companies if they were not covered with reinsurance companies (Table 8.1).

More than 200,000 people died due to earthquake in Haiti in 2010. Floods in 2010 affected around 134 million people in China and 20 million in Pakistan. In 9/11 attacks, USD 39.4 billion were paid by insurance companies in life, property and liability claims (Insurance Information Institute, 2011). Expectation of such big loses compel the companies to group together and collectively contribute to compensation.

Therefore, two or more companies collectively cover large risks through re-takaful which is a coverage taken by a takaful company from a re-takaful. Both companies agree the conditions upon which the re-takaful would share the contribution losses. Re-takaful company is paid a re-takaful *contribution* by takaful company. In this process, the takaful company is called ceding company, while the other company is called re-takaful company. Re-takaful companies also cover their risk with other companies called retrocessionaire. Takaful plays a role of financial shock absorbers in the economy and helps by way of compensations when anything goes wrong. Re-takaful plays the same role of shock absorbers for takaful companies.

Table 8.1 Large losses due to natural disasters

S. No.	*Storm and hurricane*	*Year*	*Loss in billions of USD*
1	Katrina	2005	43.6
2	Wilma	2005	10.9
3	Rita	2005	06
4	Andrew	1992	22.9

Source: Aon (2011)

Every takaful and re-takaful company decides their limit of coverage. Such limit is called their retention limit which is decided in light of available claim funds with them and nature of risk. When required coverage exceeds retention limit of a company, the said company approaches re-takaful company for the extra coverage.

The History of Reinsurance and Re-takaful

The concept of reinsurance was introduced in the seventeenth century in commercial insurance. The first known reinsurance document can be traced back to 1370 AD.[1] Reinsurance became a common practice in the nineteenth century. At that time, no companies specialised in reinsurance. Instead, ordinary insurance companies would open reinsurance branches. Cologne Re is considered to be the first reinsurance company established in 1846 (Institute and Faculty of Actuaries).

Shariah Objections Against Reinsurance

As mentioned earlier, takaful companies were established in 1979 and onwards, and they had to rely on reinsurance companies for their services. Like insurance, Islamic scholars also object to reinsurance on same religious grounds that it contains riba, uncertainty and gambling. Therefore, scholars normally don't allow takaful companies to avail their services.

After the establishment of takaful companies, re-takaful companies were also established, and they also follow the models of mudarabah and wakalah as adopted by takaful companies.

Therefore, re-takaful companies were established for providing re-takaful services to takaful companies. In 2014, 25 re-takaful and 201 operators were operating globally (World Takaful Report, 2016). Following are the re-takaful companies and their date of establishments:

- 1983—Saudi Islamic Takaful and Re-takaful Company, Bahamas
- 1985—Islamic Insurance and Reinsurance Company, Bahrain/Saudi Arabia
- 1985—B.E.S.T. Re, Tunisia

[1] D.M. Holland, 'A brief history of reinsurance', *Reinsurance News*, 65 (February 2009), p. 7.

- 1997—ASEAN Re-takaful International, Malaysia
- 2005—Takaful Re, Dubai
- 2006—Al-Fajer Re-takaful Insurance Co., Kuwait
- 2006/2007—Tokio Marine Re-takaful, Singapore
- 2006/2007—Lloyd's Re-takaful Syndicate, UK

Moreover, several reinsurance companies established their re-takaful divisions for catering demands of re-takaful, and a few of them are as follows:

- Swiss Re
- Mitsui Sumitomo
- Hannover Re
- Kuwait Re
- Trust Re

Re-takaful and reinsurance companies provide their services to almost all the continents and help in geographical spreading of risks. For example, Swiss Re, a Swiss-based life reinsurance company, provides its reinsurance facilities to majority of life insurance companies working in different countries. The ceding companies collect premiums from their clients and transfer some of their premium and risks to reinsurance companies. Now, it has established a re-takaful division for providing re-takaful facilities to many family takaful operators working in different countries.

Let's explain the reinsurance process with the help of a case study:

Case Study 8.1 Re-takaful

Person A owns a factory and wants to arrange takaful cover. The value of the factory, including the building, machinery and stock, is USD 100 million. Person A approaches a takaful operator and asks it to cover the factory against the risks of fire, including supplementary cover for earthquake, fire and shock and flooding. Retention limit of the company is Rs 25 million, as it has funds with which it can safely provide cover up to USD 25 million. Therefore, the takaful operator has two options:

(*continued*)

Case Study 8.1 (continued)

1. Offer takaful up to an amount of USD 25 million, with the rest remaining uncovered. Here, 25 million will be the retention limit of the company. As a result, Person A may ask another company to provide full cover.
2. Arrange additional cover of USD 75 million from a re-takaful company.

The takaful operator can go for the second option if it has re-takaful arrangements with other companies. If it has such arrangements in place, it arranges re-takaful cover of USD 75 million from a re-takaful company and offers cover of USD 100 million to Person A.

In this example, the takaful operator has covered 25% of the total assets of the factory, while the other 75% has been covered by a re-takaful company. On the face of it, the cover of USD 100 million will be provided by the takaful operator, which will receive the contribution in full from the factory owner. Let's say that the contribution fixed by the takaful operator is USD 5 million. The takaful operator may retain 25% of the contribution and transfer the remaining 75% to the re-takaful company. Accordingly, if Person A makes a claim, the takaful operator will pay the claim in full but will ask the re-takaful company to provide 75% of the claim amount. The re-takaful company will pay this 75% to the takaful operator, not to Person A.

Two takaful companies can also share their risk; we call this process co-takaful as none of these companies are re-takaful companies. A re-takaful company doesn't provide coverage directly to an individual client but only provides its services to takaful companies. We can say that re-takaful is a type of cover that one takaful company arranges with another takaful company as a risk-management technique.

Why Have Re-takaful Arrangements?

Among takaful operators, there are two main objectives for putting in place re-takaful arrangements.

Increasing Underwriting Capacities

The first motive is that takaful operators want to increase their capacity to accept risks in order to increase their gains. When direct takaful operators arrange re-takaful, the relationship is between the takaful operator and the re-takaful company. The participant does not have any rights in relation to the re-takaful company; the participant's relationship is only with the takaful operator that has agreed to cover the participant's risks.

Enhancing Claim Payment Abilities

The second is when the takaful operator is unable to cover property that has a very high financial value, such as large aeroplanes or factories, luxury buildings and very large shops. If an event covered occurred, paying the claim would be beyond the financial capacity of the takaful operator. Therefore, these takaful operators put re-takaful arrangements in place in order to overcome serious risks that threaten their ability to survive.

Types of Re-takaful

There are two basic methods of re-takaful: facultative and treaty. These are explained in the following section.

1. *Facultative Re-takaful*

This is the oldest method of providing re-takaful. The takaful operator must present to the re-takaful company each risk that requires re-takaful. Each risk must be presented individually, with a summary of all the basic information related to the risk. This enables the re-takaful company to decide whether or not to accept each risk that is presented to it.

2. *Treaty Re-takaful*

Using this method, a contract is made between the takaful operator and the re-takaful company in which both companies agree to work within certain financial, geographical and time limits.

The re-takaful company agrees to accept all the risks to which the conditions of the agreement apply. In return, the takaful operator commits to pass to the re-takaful company all the risks that meet those conditions. In this way, the takaful operator is able to provide takaful cover for any risk it wants to cover, as long as it is within the limits of the re-takaful agreement.

The re-takaful company cannot refuse any risk mentioned in the re-takaful agreement: it must accept all the risks presented to it, whether they are good or bad. The re-takaful company's most important criteria for accepting a re-takaful agreement are:

- The efficiency of the takaful operator's administration
- Its methods of practising takaful
- Its experience in evaluating the risk
- Its reputation in the field of takaful

The aforementioned two broad categories can be further divided as under:

Proportional Re-takaful

In proportional re-takaful, takaful company decides its retention limit in terms of amount or percentage of risk to be retained in each coverage while share the rest of the risk with the re-takaful company.

Non-proportional

Non-proportional re-takaful focuses on the loss instead of sum covered of the coverage. Therefore, re-takaful company compensates a ceding company when its claim(s) increases from a specified amount.

Issues and Challenges Faced by Re-takaful Companies

Re-takaful industry is presently facing several issues. First, retrocessions are not available, which is reducing the capacity of re-takaful companies

Second, investment opportunities are still less, which is affecting entry of new market players. Third, trained human resource is not sufficient. Re-takaful industry has to work on these challenges which, if ignored, will limit their growth in size and number, thus affecting the growth of takaful globally.

Chapter Summary

For better risk mitigation, takaful operators often share their risk with re-takaful companies. Re-takaful companies also use wakalah and mudarabah models for their operations. Takaful companies arrange re-takaful for increasing their underwriting and claim-paying capacities. There are two broad types of re-takaful agreements, namely, facultative and treaty re-takaful, which have further subtypes including proportional and non-proportional.

CHAPTER 9

Distribution Channels

Abstract This chapter has explained the distribution channels that insurance and takaful companies use. To cater to the needs of all segments of the market, companies explore all the available distribution channels for reaching out to potential clients. Traditionally, full-time exclusive agents marketed the products of a single company. Over time, independent agents and brokers entered the market, advising clients on the most suitable products available from a range of providers. These agents and brokers represent their client (either individual or corporate) in their dealings with insurance and takaful companies. Developments in information technology have opened several new channels of distribution. Use of these new channels—also called additional or alternate distribution channels—is increasing day by day. They include the Internet, banks and direct mail. In bancassurance and banca-takaful, companies use the banking platform to distribute their products. This significantly reduces marketing costs and gives banks the opportunity to earn income from fees.

Keywords Agents • Alternate distribution channels • Brokers • Banca-takaful • Distribution channels • Exclusive

A. Malik, K. Ullah, *Introduction to Takaful*,
https://doi.org/10.1007/978-981-32-9016-7_9

After reading this chapter, you should understand:

- The distribution channels used by insurance and takaful companies to market their services
- Traditional distribution channels, including exclusive agents, independent agents and brokers
- Additional alternative distribution channel(s)—ADC, including the Internet and banca-takaful

Introduction

Distribution (or product placement) is an important element of the marketing mix. Insurance and takaful companies are keen to develop different ways to deliver services effectively to clients. It is a common perception in the market that insurance is not purchased but is sold. Potential clients are often contacted by salespeople trying to convince them of the benefits of insurance. Salespeople strive to influence people to use the services provided by their company. With recent developments in technology, companies are exploring new avenues to reach potential clients.

In this chapter we will discuss the traditional and emerging alternate distribution channels used by insurance and takaful companies to approach potential customers.

Traditional Distribution Channels

There are three traditional distribution channels[1]:

- Exclusive agents (direct sales force)
- Independent agents
- Brokers

Exclusive Agents

Since the early days of insurance, companies have used the services of exclusive agents to distribute their services and products. Exclusive agents work for one insurance company only. They represent the company when

[1] R.F. Abbott, *A manager's guide to newsletters: communicating for results.* Airdrie, Canada: Word Engines Press, 1999.

dealing with clients. In life insurance companies, depending on the size of the company and the size of the market, these agents work in a team with three or more hierarchies. Hierarchies are also more common in family takaful companies. These hierarchies may include a salesperson, sales manager, area manager, regional manager and head of sales. The senior team participants provide technical support to the salesperson. Exclusive agents are also called captives.

To establish the relationship, the company and the individual sign an agent–principal agreement. This governs their relationship from that point onwards. The agreement sets out the roles and responsibilities of both parties.

Usually, a salesperson approaches a potential client to introduce the company. After identifying the potential client's financial needs, the salesperson suggests a suitable product that would meet those needs. The salesperson gives the client various illustrations to explain how the products work. If the potential client is convinced, they choose the cover and make the necessary payments.

In non-life cover, there are usually no formal teams, and salespeople work alone for the company.

Independent Agents

Independent agents provide their services to more than one company. They identify the potential client's needs and provide the most suitable product among those offered by all the companies. In their dealings with insurance companies, they represent the client.

Brokers

Brokers are registered firms that provide expertise to individuals and businesses. They represent the client in their dealings with insurance companies. Like independent agents, they look at the products on offer from a range of companies and suggest the one that best meets the needs of the potential client. The largest insurance brokers in the world, by revenue, are Marsh & McLennan, Aon Corporation, Arthur J. Gallagher & Co. and the Willis Group.[2] A broker may specialise in one or more classes of insurance or takaful.

[2] [Author], *Financial services fact book*. Insurance Information Institute, 2009.

Alternative Distribution Channels

With the development of information technology, companies have explored new channels for distributing their insurance and takaful products. These channels include:

- The Internet[3]
- Banks
- Direct mail

The Internet

Today, companies provide the facilities for clients to buy and receive quotations for services online. Several companies also provide online claims services. To make better use of the Internet, companies are investing in making their websites more user-friendly. Some companies also offer live chat, where clients can talk to company representatives online; this strengthens the company's ability to communicate with potential customers. Company's use of social media is also increasing.

The increasing use of mobile devices (tablets and smartphones) has increased the use of online services. Companies are also using social media to advertise themselves and their products.

Banks (Banca-Takaful)

Put simply, banca-takaful (also referred to as bank takaful) is the distribution of takaful products through a bank's distribution channels. A country's demographic profile influences the kind of products that are distributed through banca-takaful; its economic circumstances will determine trends in turnover and market share, and its legislative climate will determine the periphery within which banca-takaful has to operate.

In the banca-takaful model, there is a working relationship between a bank and a takaful operator (legally a principal–agent relationship where bank is an agent of insurance/takaful provider). The takaful operator uses

[3] M. Bhattad, *Trends in insurance channels* [pdf], Capgemini, retrieved 28 October 2016 from www.capgemini.com/resource-file-access/resource/pdf/Trends_in_Insurance_Channels.pdf.

the bank's marketing channels in order to offer and provide takaful products, which enables the takaful operator to reach the bank's client base.

There is a natural synergy between banks and takaful operators (or insurance companies). More than 60% of family takaful cover is now sold through banks, and most takaful companies have links with banks. Some of the advantages of banca-takaful are as follows.

- Banks have a very positive image.
- The model provides quick, fee-based income for banks.
- It enables banks to further increase their offering and meet all customers' financial needs under one roof.
- It enhances customer loyalty, as takaful contracts have a long duration.

For banks, banca-takaful is a means of diversifying their products and providing a source of additional income from fees. Takaful operators see banca-takaful as a tool for increasing their market penetration and the volume of contributions they receive. To the customer, banca-takaful gives them convenient access to a high-quality product at a reduced price. Everyone is a winner (Table 9.1).

Cover Offered Through Banca-Takaful

Another extension of bancassurance/banca-takaful model is a triparty arrangement. In triparty arrangement, third party is made part of the distribution agreements (which usually were between two parties, bank and the insurance/takaful provider). Now the question is, 'What is the need of a third party in a normal two-party arrangement?' From experience we know that third party usually brings the following benefits:

Table 9.1 Benefits of banca-takaful

Benefits for the bank	*Benefits for the takaful operator*	*Benefits for the client*
• Income from fees • Strengthens long-term client relationship • Compete more successfully in the market	• Build relationships with new clients • Higher 'hit rate' means a lower acquisition cost • Low-cost contribution collection	• Better value products • One-stop shop

1. Focus: The third-party provider usually keeps bancassurance as its core business with exclusive arrangements with the takaful provider focusing solely on distribution of product.
2. Technology: From a takaful provider's perspective, the third party brings in its own technologically enabled distribution platform where the products become bankable. For example, when takaful is linked with investment, the overall investment and fintech platforms made the takaful more accessible to potential client.
3. Innovative products and re-takaful arrangements: The arrangement brings in innovation from international markets and re-takaful limits and processes to complement the product and technology platform.

Credit Takaful

Credit takaful can be offered in cases where the bank grants a loan to the client. It serves as an additional security for the bank and protects the client's property financially if the client dies before the loan has been repaid. Health cover is also offered to participants.

Credit takaful is suitable for bank products based on murabaha, ijarah and salam, among others. The murabaha cost-plus sale model is commonly used for arranging Islamic working capital finance. Ijarah is an Islamic alternative to a lease, in which one party provides usufruct (right of use) of assets or human resources to another party. Salam is an advance sale in which the price is fixed and the delivery is made on a future date; Shariah allows it for a few restricted commodities.

Depositors' Takaful

In depositors' takaful, the client is provided with death cover with a sum assured that is equal to a certain multiple of their deposits in the bank. Banks always provide this cover free of charge as an incentive to encourage clients to deposit more money in a particular bank. It can be offered with any savings account, but a minimum deposit amount is usually required. The level of cover is usually determined by factors such as price of the cover and underwriting.

The contribution is usually paid by the bank, but it can also be paid by the depositor.

ATM Cash Withdrawal Cover

Some banks also offer cover against theft to customers who make cash withdrawals from their ATMs. If someone snatches the money withdrawn by a client within a specific geographical area, the client can make a claim, and the bank will compensate the client through their partner takaful operator.

Direct Mail

Companies also send direct mail to potential customers with information about their products and services. Takaful and insurance companies sometimes outsource their direct mailing process to companies that specialise in direct mail campaigns.

Chapter Summary

This chapter has explained the distribution channels that insurance and takaful companies use. To cater to the needs of all segments of the market, companies explore all the available distribution channels for reaching out to potential clients.

Traditionally, full-time exclusive agents marketed the products of a single company. Over time, independent agents and brokers entered the market, advising clients on the most suitable products available from a range of providers. These agents and brokers represent their client (either individual or corporate) in their dealings with insurance and takaful companies.

Developments in information technology have opened up several new channels of distribution. Use of these new channels—also called additional or alternate distribution channels—is increasing day by day. They include the Internet, banks and direct mail. In bancassurance and banca-takaful, companies use the banking platform to distribute their products. This significantly reduces marketing costs and gives banks the opportunity to earn income from fees.

CHAPTER 10

Underwriting Management

Abstract This chapter has focused on analysing the risks that potential participants bring to the takaful fund. This is done through a process called underwriting, in which a professional underwriter assesses each potential participant's eligibility for cover. Based on the risk analysis, the underwriter selects participants of the takaful fund, classifies them according to the risk they present and decides their contributions. Participants are placed into different classes of risk namely preferred, standard, substandard (rated) and declined. Underwriters follow a risk-analysis process that involves collecting and analysing information. After carrying out the analysis, the underwriter can accept the takaful application, refuse the request for cover or accept the application but attach conditions to the cover. If the underwriter approves the application, it is forwarded to the participant membership department for completion. If the application is refused, a rejection letter will be sent to the takaful agent or consultant and the applicant. If modifications need to be made, the application will be sent back to the takaful agent, who will review it with the potential participant.

Keywords Analysis of risk • Participant membership • Underwriting

A. Malik, K. Ullah, *Introduction to Takaful*,
https://doi.org/10.1007/978-981-32-9016-7_10

After reading this chapter, you should understand:

- What an underwriter is
- The different types of underwriters
- The process of underwriting in different classes of takaful, including life, health, motor, buildings, cash and marine

Introduction

The operations of takaful companies are based on taking contributions from participants and paying claims when an event that is covered occurs. The contributions collected should be equitable; that is, they should be in proportion to the risk that each participant brings to the takaful fund.

The takaful underwriter is responsible for:

- Allowing potential participants to join the takaful fund only if they bring an acceptable level of risk.
- Fixing each participant's contributions in accordance with the risk they present.
- Arranging for a participant membership document (PMD) to be issued to participants. The PMD contains details of the cover available to the participant.

What Is Takaful (Insurance) Underwriting?

Underwriting in takaful is the process of assessing an applicant's eligibility for the takaful cover they have requested. It involves selecting and classifying applicants for takaful and deciding their contributions.

Sound underwriting is a must for the stability of the takaful fund.

A statement of underwriting policy establishes underwriting strategies that are consistent with the company's objectives, such as:

- Acceptable classes of business
- Classifying risk appropriately
- The maximum and minimum sum assured that can be allowed for a single participant
- Arranging re-takaful

History of the Term

The term insurance underwriter originated in marine insurance.[1] Merchants who were willing to take on a portion of the risk of a voyage would list how much they were willing to cover and sign their names under a line at the bottom of a contract.[2] They became known as underwriters because they wrote their names under the contract terms. Underwriters are responsible for evaluating the risks associated with potential participants. Using the risk and exposure data they gather, underwriters determine what cover an insurer can offer a client and how much should be the premium.

The underwriter will also decide if the risk that a potential participant presents is too high for the takaful operator to accept. The underwriter's role is to protect the takaful fund from risks that will almost certainly lead to a loss. Underwriting is an absolute necessity in the takaful application process, as it is a means to correctly place applicants into appropriate risk classes.

By grouping potential participants into appropriate risk classes, takaful operators are able to make contributions affordable for the majority of the participants. The risk class that a potential participant is placed in is determined by a variety of factors. Each risk class is composed of individuals and companies with similar characteristics. These classes may vary from company to company, depending on their underwriting strategies and policies. Here is a concept of a risk classification system.

- *Preferred Potential Participants*—Preferred participants are ideal, as they present the lowest risk. Because of this, the underwriter usually charges them the lowest contribution rates. On a continuum of risk, they represent the safest category of potential takaful participants.
- *Standard Potential Participants*—Participants in this class are usually charged the standard contribution rate because they bring an average level of risk to the takaful fund.
- *Substandard Potential Participants (also known as 'rated')*—Participants in this class are usually charged more than those in the standard class.
- *Declined*—Applicants in this class have a risk that cannot be covered or that lies outside the company's acceptable range.

[1] J. Hebron, 'Where the term "underwriting" comes from', *The Basis Point*, 28 October 2012, retrieved 28 October 2016 from http://thebasispoint.com/2012/10/28/where-the-term-underwriting-comes-from/.

[2] E. Wertheimer, *Underwriting: the poetics of insurance in America, 1722–1872*. Stanford, CA: Stanford University Press, 2006.

Table 10.1 Examples of risk classifications

No.	*Client risk profile*	*Underwriting class*
1	An athlete who is applying for a life cover.	Preferred
2	A person who has been involved in a fraudulent claim for the theft of a vehicle and who is applying for motor cover.	Declined
3	A person who has diabetes (within the acceptable range for a family takaful operator) and is applying for life cover.	Substandard
5	An office worker who has a normal weight and height with no family history of early natural deaths and is applying for life cover.	Standard
6	A person who is employed by the police whose duties involve fieldwork and who is applying for life cover.	Substandard

Table 10.1 provides some examples of risk classification. As mentioned earlier, classification systems may vary from company to company, depending on their underwriting policy.

The Role of Takaful Consultants in Underwriting

A takaful consultant usually provides all the information about a potential participant that is needed to accurately assess their membership of the fund. This assessment ensures that the type of takaful membership, the sum assured and the contribution are appropriate for the applicant. The takaful consultant has a key role in advising applicants to take out cover that they can afford. Failing to get this right can result in participants taking out inappropriate cover that they may not be able to afford in future.

Deciding Takaful Contributions

This refers to calculating the applicant's contribution for their desired takaful cover. The takaful contribution is worked out based on a rate per exposure unit.

The takaful contribution is calculated as follows:

$$\text{Contribution} = \text{mortality rate} \times \text{exposure units}$$

The total contributions charged to all participants must add up to enough to enable the takaful fund to pay all claims and expenses during the policy period.

The rates and contributions are determined by an actuary, using the company's past loss experience and industry statistics.

Let's explain this with the help of a case study.

Case Study 10.1 Determining Rates and Contributions

A takaful operator needs to set the contribution rate for a specific group of participants as follows.

Number of participants: 100 (A)

Desired family term takaful cover for each participant: USD 1000 (B)

Duration of cover: One year

Age of all participants: 35 years

Mortality rate for people aged 35: 10 deaths a year for every 1000 people.

Total number of expected claims (based on the mortality rate): 10 (C)

Amount needed to pay 10 claims: (B × C) = USD 10,000 (D)

Contribution rate per client (considering cost of paying claims only)

Amount required to pay claims: (D ÷ A) = USD 100

This calculation shows that by collecting USD 100 from all 100 clients, the takaful fund will be able to pay USD 1000 to each of the 10 families making a claim.

Therefore, the contribution rate per USD 1000 of cover is USD 100 for a 35-year-old person, and one exposure unit is USD 1000.

Using the contribution rate to calculate the contribution based on the sum assured

If a client wants to arrange cover for USD 10,000, their contribution will be calculated by multiplying the rate per USD 1000 by the number of exposure units requested:

Contribution = rate (USD 100) × exposure units (10) = USD 1000

In this example, the rate per USD 1000 is 100, and the number of units is 10, so we multiplied 100 by 10. In the same way, larger sums assured for the same age group can be calculated using the same rate of USD 100 for every USD 1000 of cover requested.

Process of Underwriting

The steps involved in underwriting are usually mentioned in the takaful operator's underwriting manual or guidelines. These may differ for each company, but the general process is essentially the same. The steps in the underwriting process are as follows.

Step 1: Information Collection

Collecting information is the first step in the underwriting process. The underwriter needs several key pieces of information in order to accurately evaluate the potential participant. This information will vary depending on the type of takaful cover being applied for. For instance, in motor takaful, the underwriter may need to know the following.

- *The make and model of the vehicle.* Parts for some vehicles are more expensive than those of others.
- *The owner's driving history.* This provides information about the driver's level of care and expertise.
- *The owner's address.* In some areas, the risk of accidents or theft may be higher.

Step 2: Assessment of the Collected Information

After gathering all the information needed, the underwriter begins to analyse it. The underwriter follows the specific underwriting guidelines that the takaful operator has provided in order to evaluate all the information that has been collected.

- There are different levels of authority among underwriters. If, after analysing the information, the underwriter determines that a decision needs to be made by an underwriter who has the necessary authority, they will pass the information on to the appropriate underwriter.
- The purpose of analysing the information is to assess the level of risk that a potential participant will transfer to the takaful operator's takaful fund.
- Using the earlier example of motor takaful, a driver who has a clean driving record and good credit is usually preferable to a driver who has several driving infractions or accidents on their record.

Step 3: Application of the Appropriate Option

After analysing the information, the underwriter identifies which option to choose. These options are related to the risk class that a potential participant has been placed in and are as follows.

- *Approve issuing a policy by accepting the takaful application.* If the underwriter approves the application, it will be forwarded to the applicable PMD processing department for completion.
- *Refuse the applicant's request for cover.* If the application is refused, a rejection letter will be issued to the takaful agent and the applicant.
- *Accept the application for cover, but attach specific conditions.* If modifications need to be made, the application will be sent back to the takaful agent, who will discuss it with the potential participant. Contribution may increase depending on the risk profile of the proposed participant.

Reasons of Delay in Finalising the Option

The time it takes to complete the underwriting process can vary widely depending on several factors. For cases with few requirements, the entire process may take as little as one or two days. For more complicated cases, it can take much longer.

One important factor that prolongs the underwriting process is trouble verifying the information provided by the applicant. Applicants can reduce how long the process takes by providing as much information and documentation as possible. This means the underwriter will not have to spend as much time looking for the information they need.

Underwriting is a vital tool used by the takaful operator to assess the risks of potential participants and set contribution rates that reflect the risks being transferred to the takaful fund.

Ultimately, underwriting benefits the takaful operator and its participants by keeping contributions to a minimum and reducing the risk of loss.

Types of Underwriter

A takaful operator may offer many different types of cover. Therefore, the following different types of underwriters are needed.

Life Underwriter

Life underwriters underwrite only family takaful, which includes cover for individuals and groups. The events covered are usually the death or injury of a participant.

Health Underwriter

Health underwriters underwrite cover related to outpatient services and hospitalisation.

Commercial Property Underwriter

Commercial property underwriters specialise in buildings used for commercial purposes, such as factories, shopping centres and offices.

Automobile Underwriter

Automobile underwriters specialise in motor cover, including cover for light- and heavy-duty private and commercial vehicles.

Marine Underwriter

Marine underwriters underwrite cover for goods being transported from one place to another by sea, air, rail and road.

Professional Liability Underwriter

Through professional liability takaful, a professional (for instance, a medical doctor or a lawyer) passes on their risk of liability if they make a mistake when providing a professional service and their client suffers a loss as a result. For example, a surgeon could make a mistake during an operation on a patient that results in the patient's death. The patient's family may sue the surgeon in a court of law. If the surgeon is found guilty and is ordered to pay compensation to the family, the takaful operator will pay the compensation to the patient's family on the surgeon's behalf.

Professional liability takaful is a very expensive product. However, in many countries, some professionals are not allowed to practise until they have arranged professional liability takaful or insurance.

While underwriting professional liability takaful, the underwriters must be able to gather and understand the various documents used to evaluate each application and determine whether the applicant meets the operator's underwriting standards.

Such documents may include site-inspection reports and business or personal financial statements.

Product Liability Underwriter

If someone is injured or suffers some other loss caused by using a product, that person may sue the manufacturer of the product. If the manufacturer is found guilty, the court may order them to pay damages or compensation to the customer. However, if the manufacturer has product liability takaful, the takaful operator will pay the compensation and damages.

Product liability underwriters must be able to evaluate how likely past losses, judgements and settlements are to happen again in order to determine the relative future risk. To do this accurately, they have to be familiar with current trends in court judgements and with liability laws.

Group Underwriter

Many types of takaful are written on a group basis; for example, group life and health takaful are often written in this manner. Group takaful is handled somewhat differently from individual policies when it comes to underwriting.

In general, in group life and health takaful, a rate is established that applies to the entire group to be covered. This rate is decided by analysing the characteristics of the group as a whole and the characteristics of individuals within the group. The rate is usually reviewed and revised once a year.

Factors Assessed in Family Takaful Underwriting

Each class of takaful has its own key factors that are evaluated for underwriting purposes. As mentioned at the beginning of this chapter, the underwriter has to decide on the contribution for every participant based on the risk that each participant brings to the takaful fund. Such a contribution is also called takaful contribution. In family takaful, such as life, health and disability cover, multiple factors are used in the underwriting process. These factors have a significant impact on how much risk a person brings to the takaful fund. Therefore, underwriters have to consider them when deciding whether the takaful operator should provide cover and how much the applicant should contribute. Following are details of the important factors:

Age

In family takaful, the contribution rate is strongly linked to the applicant's mortality rate. In takaful, the ***mortality rate*** (or ***death rate***) is a measure of the number of deaths in a particular age group for a particular size of that population in a period of time. The mortality rate increases with age. Family takaful operators are especially interested in knowing about the number of deaths in a particular age group. Let's explain how this works with the help of a case study.

Case Study 10.2 Age

Consider a group of 1000 men aged 45.

Suppose the average mortality rate, according to the mortality table, is 15 men in every 1000. Therefore, the expected number of deaths among 1000 men aged 45 is 15 per year.

So, if a takaful operator has issued life cover of USD 100,000 to those 1000 men and 15 participants die, the total claims payable to the beneficiaries of these 15 participants will be:

USD 100,000 × 15 = USD 1,500,000

Therefore, the takaful company needs at least USD 1500,000 to pay 15 beneficiaries a sum assured of USD 100,000. To achieve this, the takaful company must take at least USD 1500 from each of the 1000 men aged 45.

USD 150,000 ÷ 1000 = USD 150.

Gender

The mortality rate among women is less than it is among men. For example, the mortality rate among women aged 35 may be 8 per 1000, while among men of the same age it may be 10 per 1000. Therefore, the contribution for a woman aged 35 will be less than the contribution for a man aged 35.

Health and Health History

In health takaful, the contribution rate is strongly associated with the morbidity rate, which is the frequency at which a disease appears in a population. Women have a higher morbidity rate than men, so women have to make a higher contribution for the same amount of health takaful. For knowing the medical condition of a client, the company may ask for medical examination and diagnostic tests, collectively called medical requirements which increase with age and face value.

You may find the following chart helpful for understanding the medical requirements normally required by the company. The trend is towards reducing medical requirements (Exhibit 10.1).

Occupation and Employment History

People working in dangerous professions have a higher risk of death and injury than people working in other professions. For example, a person operating a crane in a hilly area will face more risk than a person working in an office. Therefore, based on the principle of equitable contributions, the crane operator has to pay more than the office worker for the same amount of cover.

Financial Circumstances

The underwriter should approve takaful cover only if it is in line with the applicant's financial circumstances. A client who wants to take out life cover that is higher than his/her financial status suggests they need (e.g., a security guard with an annual salary of USD 14,000 applying for life takaful cover with face value of USD 500,000 and an annual contribution

LIFE UNDERWRITING REQUIREMENTS CHART

Sum at Risk in US$	← Age Groups → 18-35	36-40	41-45	46-50	51-55	56-60	61-65
Up to 3000	Non-Medical	Non- Medical	Non- Medical	Non- Medical	Non- Medical	MR	MR, PUR, ECG, BS, CXR
3001 to 6000	Non-Medical	Non- Medical	Non- Medical	Non- Medical	MR	MR, PUR, ECG	MR, PUR, ECG, BS, CXR
6001 to 7500	Non- Medical	Non- Medical	Non- Medical	Non- Medical	MR, PUR, ECG	MR, PUR, ECG	MR, PUR, Ex-ECG, BS, CXR
7501 to 9000	Non- Medical	Non- Medical	Non- Medical	MR PUR	MR, PUR, ECG	MR, PUR, ECG	MR, PUR, Ex-ECG, BS, CXR
9001 to 12000	Non- Medical	Non- Medical	MR PUR	MR PUR	MR, PUR, Ex-ECG, BS, SGPT	MR, PUR, Ex-ECG, BS	MR, PUR, Ex-ECG, BS, CXR
12001 to 15000	Non- Medical	Non- Medical	MR PUR FBS	MR, PUR, FBS, Ex-ECG	MR, PUR, Ex-ECG, BS, SGPT	MR, PUR, Ex-ECG, BS	MR, PUR, Ex-ECG, BS, CXR
15001 to 25000	Non- Medical	MR PUR	MR, PUR, FBS, Ex-ECG	MR, PUR, Ex-ECG, BS, SGPT	MR, PUR, Ex-ECG, BS, SGPT	MR, PUR, Ex-ECG, BS, SGPT	MR, PUR, Ex-ECG, BS, SGPT, CXR
25001 to 30000	MR PUR	MR, PUR, Ex-ECG, BS, SGPT	MR, PUR, Ex-ECG, BS, SGPT	MR, PUR, Ex-ECG, BS, SGPT	MR, PUR, Ex-ECG, BS, SGPT	MR, PUR, Ex-ECG, BS, SGPT	MR, PUR, Ex-ECG, BS, SGPT, CXR
30001 to 50000	MR, PUR, Ex-ECG, BS, SGPT	MR, PUR, Ex-ECG, BS, SGPT	MR, PUR, Ex-ECG, BS, SGPT	MR, PUR, Ex-ECG, BS, SGPT	MR, PUR, Ex-ECG, BS, SGPT	MR, PUR, Ex-ECG, BS, SGPT	MR, PUR, Ex-ECG, BS, SGPT, CXR
50001 to 99, 999	MR, PUR, Ex-ECG, BS, LFT, HEPATITIS B & C	MR, PUR, Ex-ECG, BS, LFT, HEPATITIS B & C	MR, PUR, Ex-ECG, BS, LFT, HEPATITIS B & C	MR, PUR, Ex-ECG, BS, LFT, HEPATITIS B & C	MR, PUR, Ex-ECG, BS, LFT, HEPATITIS B & C	MR, PUR, Ex-ECG, BS, LFT, HEPATITIS B & C	MR, PUR, Ex-ECG, BS, LFT, CXR, HEPATITIS B & C

Exhibit 10.1 Underwriting requirements chart

100000 & above	MR, PUR, Ex-ECG, BS, LFT, SERUM CREATININE, HEPATITIS B & C, LIPID PROFILE, CHEST X-RAY, HIV
Blood Studies (BS)	Fasting Blood Sugar (FBS), CBC, ESR, S. Cholesterol, S.Urea
Liver Function Test (LFTs)	Serum Bilirubin (Direct & Indirect), SGPT, SGOT, Gama GT, Alkaline Phosphatase
Lipid Profile	Total Lipids, S. Cholesterol, Triglycerides, HDL, LDL

*Note:

1. For Ages over 60 and for substandard lives over 55, special conditions shall apply as prescribed in Underwriting Guidelines.
2. For re-takaful business, the sum at risk (SAR) be calculated and medical requirements be followed in the manner as prescribed in Underwriting Guidelines.
3. Proposals attracting facultative re-takaful business, ETT on Bruce Protocol shall be required.

Exhibit 10.1 (continued)

of USD 50,000 for 15 years) may alert the underwriter. In high sum assured or higher age of the proposed participant, the underwriter should ask for proof of income to justify the high sum assured; if the applicant cannot provide proof, the underwriter should reject the application or suggest reducing the sum assured.

If someone applies for cover that is not in line with their financial circumstances, this may present a moral hazard.

Personal Habits

Some habits, such as smoking or drinking alcohol, have a negative effect on health. Therefore, underwriters may set a higher contribution for participants with certain habits.

Sum Covered of the Policy

The contribution rate is linked to the amount of cover requested, and it increases as the sum assured increases. A person requesting life cover for USD 100,000 will pay less than a person requesting life cover for USD 1 million.

Let's look at some case studies of contribution calculations in group and individual family takaful to clarify how this is affected by the aforementioned factors.

Case Study 10.3 Group Family Takaful

A takaful operator wants to calculate participant contributions for the following group family takaful scheme.

Number of clients to be covered: 10,000 (A)

Sum assured: USD 100,000 (B)

Mortality rate: 21 deaths a year in every 10,000 people (C)

Total claim amount payable in one year: (C × B) = USD 2.1 million (D)

Contribution to be charged to every client: (D ÷ A) = USD 210

Therefore, the calculation shows that every participant needs to pay USD 210 a year to the takaful operator to enable the operator to pay death claims to the beneficiaries of 21 participants in one year.

Case Study 10.4 Individual Family Takaful

A takaful operator wants to calculate participant contributions for Person A, who has applied for individual family takaful cover.

Sum assured/Face value: USD 100,000
Duration: 19 years
Gender: Male
Age: 37 years
Profession: Engineer
Supplementary contracts (riders) requested:

- Family income benefit (FIB) at 20% for 19 years
- Accidental indemnity benefit (AIB)

The basic annual contribution rate for a sum assured of USD 1000 is USD 52.56. However, Person A has requested cover for USD 100,000. Therefore, Person A's annual contribution will be calculated as follows:

USD 100 × 52.56 = 5256 (A)
AIB rate: USD 4 per 1000
AIB contribution: USD 4 × 100 = 400 (B)
FIB rate: 20% for 19 years = 20.62
FIB contribution: 20.62 × 100 = USD 2062 (C)
Total annual contribution: (A + B + C) = USD 7718

Underwriting in General Takaful

As explained previously, cover that is not family takaful is categorised as general takaful. It includes cover for items (such as vehicles, buildings, machinery and stock) against risks (such as fire, earthquake, riots, strikes, accidents, terrorism, flooding and theft).

Here is a recap of the main features of general takaful.

- *Cover Is Usually Short Term*

Unlike family takaful, general takaful policies last for one year or less. Every year, the cover has to be renewed.

- *Contributions May Vary*

Because of changes in market value, the sum assured for items of property may increase or decrease. If a successful claim is made, the contribution may increase when the cover is renewed.

- *Principle of Indemnity*

All general takaful cover is based on principle of indemnity, which is that the participant making a claim should be returned to the same financial circumstances they were in before the loss occurred. For example, if a participant's car is stolen, the claim is paid with the intention that the participant may replace their car by buying the same kind (make and model) of car.

- *Payment of a Claim May or May Not Terminate a Contract*

Unlike family takaful cover, which ends when a participant dies and a claim is paid to the beneficiary, general takaful cover may continue. If an item of property is partly damaged, the takaful operator pays a claim of partial loss to the participant, and the cover continues until the term ends.

- *The Risk to Be Covered Does Not Necessarily Increase Over Time*

In family takaful, the mortality rate increases with each passing year, thus increasing the risk of death. In general takaful, the risk does not necessarily increase.

We discussed the types of general takaful in detail in Chap. 6. In this chapter, we will focus on underwriting management in motor, fire, marine and cash takaful.

Underwriting of Motor Takaful

Each type of takaful cover has its own risk factors that increase or decrease the likelihood and extent of loss. When underwriting motor cover, the underwriter must consider the following factors.

The Value of the Vehicle
The value of the vehicle is always an important consideration for the underwriter, because a single loss of a high-value vehicle can result in a large outflow of cash from the takaful fund. The contribution rate is always calculated as a percentage of the value of the vehicle; therefore, the contribution increases as the value of the vehicle increases. The sum assured should be equal to or close to the market value of the vehicle.

The Applicant's Driving History
If a driver has been involved in several road traffic accidents, the underwriter will place the driver in the substandard category, which usually results in the driver paying a higher contribution rate than those in the preferred or standard categories.

The Type of Cover Requested
The three main types of motor cover are as follows.

1. Third-party liability only
2. Total loss and theft
3. Comprehensive

As the scope of the cover increases from 1 to 3, so does the contribution rate.

Use of the Vehicle
Vehicles used for commercial purposes have a higher risk of being in an accident than vehicles used for domestic purposes only. Therefore, the contribution rate for commercial vehicles is higher than the contribution rate for domestic or private vehicles.

The applicant provides information about all the factors shown above by answering questions in a proposal form. The underwriter then either makes a decision or asks the applicant to provide further information.

Fire Takaful

Similar to motor underwriting, in fire takaful the underwriter must consider specific factors when deciding whether to issue cover and what the contribution rate should be. An applicant may ask for fire takaful cover for their home, business premises, stock, machinery and so on. The underwriter should consider the following factors before deciding.

The Construction of the Building

For buildings cover, the construction of the building has an important impact on how safe it is. If there is a fire or an earthquake, the roof may collapse if the building is poorly constructed, damaging anything underneath it. Therefore, the contribution rate is lower for stable constructions, as they pose less risk of loss. In contrast, the rate is higher for weaker constructions, which present more risk. The underwriter should make detailed enquiries about the construction of a building in order to make an informed decision.

The Value of the Property

The higher the value of the property, the higher the contribution will be.

The Condition of the Property

If the building, equipment or other property is not in a good condition due to its age, its construction type or lack of maintenance, the likelihood of loss is higher, which increases the contribution rate. The underwriter may refuse a request for cover if the condition of the property is very poor.

Potential Hazards Surrounding the Property

There may be establishments in the vicinity of the building to be covered that could trigger a fire, such as petrol stations or warehouses containing flammable goods. For example, a fire at a petrol station could spread to the building for which fire cover is being considered. Therefore, the contribution rate for fire takaful cover for such a building is higher than the contribution rate for buildings that do not have such establishments nearby.

Use of the Property

How an item of property (e.g., a building) is used also affects the likelihood of fire. For example, a building may be used for production purposes (such as making sausages, matchsticks or juice) that require heat and flame. Such activities increase the risk of fire. It follows that an office building where there is no production activity poses less risk of fire. Therefore, the contribution rate is higher for buildings with more risk of fire than it is for buildings with less risk.

Precautionary measures, such as better housekeeping and a focus on preventing flammable items coming into contact with fire, help to reduce the risk of fire. Measures to control and manage fire (such as fire alarms, a sprinkler system, fire hoses, water buckets and staff training) may reduce the extent of any loss caused by fire. Therefore, underwriters may offer considerable discounts to owners of buildings with such measures in place.

Prior Losses Associated with the Property

Any history of claims may also increase the contribution rate.

The applicant provides information about all the aforementioned factors by answering questions in a proposal form. The underwriter then either makes a decision or asks the applicant to provide further information.

Let's look at some case studies of underwriting for fire takaful.

Case Study 10.5 Fire Takaful for a Residential Building

Person A approaches a takaful operator to arrange fire cover for their home. The underwriter identifies the following information:

Value of the building, excluding the price of the land it stands on (sum assured): USD 50 million

Cover required: Fire and lightning (basic cover)

Allied perils: Earthquake, fire and shock; atmospheric disturbance

The takaful operator calculates Person A's annual contribution as follows.

Required cover	*Rate (USD per 100 of sum covered) (%)*	*Contribution (based on sum assured of USD 50 million)*
Fire and lightning	0.005	0.005 × USD 50 million = USD 2500
Earthquake, fire and shock	0.006	0.006 × USD 50 million = USD 3000
Atmospheric disturbance	0.001	0.001 × USD 50 million = USD 5000
Total annual contribution		USD 10,500

Case Study 10.6 Fire Cover for a Commercial Building

Company A approaches a takaful operator to arrange cover for their warehouse. The underwriter gets the following information:

Value of the building, excluding the price of the land it stands on (sum assured): USD 50 million

Cover required: Fire and lightning (basic cover)

Allied perils: Earthquake, fire and shock; atmospheric disturbance; riot and strike damage

The takaful operator calculates Company A's annual contribution as follows.

Required cover	*Rate (USD per 100 of sum covered) (%)*	*Contribution (based on sum assured of USD 50 million)*
Fire and lightning	0.001	0.001 × USD 50 million = USD 5000
Earthquake, fire and shock	0.006	0.006 × USD 50 million = USD 3000
Atmospheric disturbance	0.001	0.001 × USD 50 million = USD 5000
Riot and strike damage	0.006	0.006 × USD 50 million = USD 3000
Total annual contribution		USD 16000

Fire takaful proposal form for domestic building is displayed in Exhibit 10.2, which will further improve the understanding of fire underwriting.

Marine Takaful

In marine, cover for the following can be taken:

- Hull—structural framework of vessel
- Goods in transit

When certain goods are transported from one place to another by sea, rail, air or road, they are put at risk. Takaful cover against these risks is called marine takaful. There are three main categories of cover.

- Clause A: maximum cover
- Clause B: less cover than Clause A but more cover than Clause C
- Clause C: minimum cover

GENERAL TAKAFUL

Pak-Qatar General Takaful Limited

Suite # 402-403,
Business Arcade
Block 6, Sharea Faisal
P.E.C.H.S.,
Karachi.

Contact Details:
Phone (92 21) 34380357-61
Fax No. (92 21) 34386453
Email info@pakqatar.com.pk
Web: www.pakqatar.com.pk

Questionnaire and
Proposal form Home Takaful

Full Name ______________________________

Address ______________________________

Tel. Nos. ______________________________

Cell. No. ______________________________

Would you like to be on our SMS mailing list? ☐ Yes ☐ No

CNIC No. ______________________________

Occupation ______________________________

Address ______________________________

____

Apartment ☐

Bungalow (Sole Occupier) ☐

Bungalow (Multiple Occupations) ☐

Plot Area/Covered Area ______________________________

Construction Type:

RCC ☐ Non-RCC ☐

Security Arrangements:

Armed Response ☐ Watchman ☐

Armed Guard ☐ None ☐

Location of Locker ______________________________

Name of previous Home Insurer/Takaful Company (If Any)

____

Loss History (If any) ______________________________

Has any insurer or Takaful Company ever declined a proposal for Insurance/Takaful from you, imposed Special conditions or cancelled any policy issued to you?

____

I hereby declare that all information stated in this proposal is true and complete and that I have not concealed anything material to be known to PQGT and I hereby agree that this proposal and declaration shall be the basis of the contract betweenPQGT and me.

Date Signature of Proposer

Exhibit 10.2 Fire takaful proposal form

PARTICIPANT VALUES

Items	Values
Building	
Civil Structure (Excl. Foundations, plinths & pavements)	
Contents	
Furniture	
Upholstery	
Carpets	
Dinnerware & Crockery	
Kitchen Appliance	
Refrigerator & Deep Freezer	
Air Conditioners	
Television/Plasma Screen	
DVD/Home Theatre/Audio System	
Personal Computers	
Cameras	
Phone Sets	
Apparel	
Home Fabrics	
Personal Effects	
Other Items	
Jewellery Gold Sets	
Diamond Sets	
Rings	
Necklaces	
Earrings	
Bangles	
Cash & prize bonds	
Total Contents	

DECLARATION

1. I/We hereby confirm that the details contained in this proposal form are true and correct to the best of my/our knowledge and belief and I/We have not concealed, misrepresented or misstated any material fact. I/We further undertake to inform the company of any material alterations to these facts occurring during the currency of this Policy.

2. I/We agree that the statements and declaration contained in this proposal form shall be the basis of my/our beneficiary status in the Takaful Fund and deemed to be incorporated in the Policy.

3. I/We hereby undertake to contribute the agreed amount to the Takaful Fund maintained and operated by the company.

4. I/We understand that as per the rules of Takaful Fund, by doing so I shall stand entitled to the membership of the Takaful Fund and being one of its beneficiaries subject to the rules and regulations of the Fund.

5. As a prospective beneficiary of the Fund, I/We offer my/our property, as specifically described in the attached schedule, forthe indemnity cover provided by the Fund to its beneficiaries.

6. I/We hereby request to be issued with a confirmation to acknowledge my membership and my consequential rights as a beneficiary of the Fund.

Signed at: ____________________ Signature of the Participants: ________________

Dated: ________________ Name of Signatory: ________________________

The liability of the Company does not commence until the Proposal has been accepted and the contribution paid. Only official receipt issued from the Company on printed form is binding on the Company

Exhibit 10.2 (continued)

Let's look at a case study of underwriting goods transported by sea for the highest level of cover. A marine cargo takaful membership document is displayed at Case Study 10.7 for a better understanding.

Case Study 10.7 Importing Raw Materials from India

Company B approaches a takaful operator to arrange cover for goods being imported to Pakistan from India. The details of the cover required are as follows:

Cover: Clause A (all risks)

Mode of transport: by sea

Voyage: From any Indian seaport to Karachi seaport

Invoice value: USD 21,000 (A) (for simplification, the invoice amount is provided in USD and not in Indian rupees) plus bank charges, documentation costs and so forth at 10% of the invoice value: (A × 1.10) = USD 23,100 (B)

Conversation into local currency (USD) at an exchange rate of 105.00: (B × 105) = USD 2,425,500

Total value to be covered or sum covered: USD 2,425,500 (C)

The takaful operator calculates Company B's annual contribution as follows:

Marine cover at 0.2%: (C × 0.002) = USD 4851 (D)

War and strike, riot and civil commotion = USD 1213 (E)

Total: (D + E) = USD 6064 (F)

Add 1% federal insurance fee: (F × 0.01) = USD 61 (G)

Add 15% federal excise duty: (F × 0.15) = USD 910 (H)

Add stamp duty at 0.006% of the sum assured: (C × 0.00006) = USD 146 (I)

Total annual contribution: (F + G + H + I) = USD 7181.

Cash Takaful

When underwriting applications for cash takaful, an underwriter should consider the following.

- The situation with regard to law and order in the area to be covered.
- The safety measures taken by the applicant, such as the presence of guards in the applicant's office premises.
- The amount of cash to be transported in one vehicle.

Case Study 10.8 Cash Takaful

Supermarket Owner A wants to arrange cash takaful for cash kept in the counter, in a safe and in transit. The supermarket owner provides information to the takaful operator about the nature of the business, its location and the safety measures in place at the supermarket. For better risk management, the supermarket owner establishes protocols for keeping cash up to a value of:

- USD 50,000 at the counter
- USD 100,000 in the safe
- USD 1 million in transit

Therefore, Supermarket Owner A asks for cover against robbery for USD 50,000 at the counter, USD 100,000 in the safe and USD 1 million in transit.

The takaful operator calculates Supermarket Owner A's contribution as follows.

Required cover	*Rate (USD Per 100 of sum covered) (%)*	*Contribution (USD)*
Cash at the counter	6	6% × 50,000 = 3000
Cash in the safe	1	1% × 1,00,000 = 1000
Cash in transit	3	3% × 1 million = 30,000
Total contribution		USD 34,000

Chapter Summary

This chapter has focused on analysing the risks that potential participants bring to the takaful fund. This is done through a process called underwriting, in which a professional underwriter assesses each potential participant's eligibility for cover. Based on the risk analysis, the underwriter selects participants of the takaful fund, classifies them according to the risk they present and decides their contributions.

Participants are placed into different classes of risk namely preferred, standard, substandard (rated) and declined.

Underwriters follow a risk-analysis process that involves collecting and analysing information. After carrying out the analysis, the underwriter can:

- Accept the takaful application
- Refuse the request for cover
- Accept the application but attach conditions to the cover

If the underwriter approves the application, it is forwarded to the PMD processing department for completion. If the application is refused, a rejection letter will be sent to the takaful agent or consultant and the applicant. If modifications need to be made, the application will be sent back to the takaful agent, who will review it with the potential participant.

CHAPTER 11

Claim Management

Abstract A test for any takaful operator is how it handles claims when an event covered occurs. A thorough analysis of the claim is necessary in order to differentiate between genuine and fraudulent claims. The operator is responsible for refusing fraudulent claims and processing genuine claims swiftly. The starting steps in the process of handling claims are intimation by the participant or nominee, recording claims in the operator's books and issuing claim forms. After receiving claim intimation, the operator issues claim forms in order to establish the following: cause of loss, which should match the events covered, otherwise, the claim is not payable; extent of loss, which usually applies in general takaful claims; and whether an investigation of the claim is needed. General takaful claims are usually processed by licensed surveyors. Surveyors engage experts to assess losses relating to vehicles, buildings and machinery. Surveyors assist the takaful operator to decide whether or not the claim is payable and, if it is, the genuine amount to be paid.

Keywords Claim management • Event covered • Surveyors

After reading this chapter, you should understand:

- The process of settling claims
- Calculating family and general takaful claims
- The role of the surveyor in settling general takaful claims

A. Malik, K. Ullah, *Introduction to Takaful*,
https://doi.org/10.1007/978-981-32-9016-7_11

Introduction

Claims management is the process of determining cover and legal liability and settling claims. The main objective of claims management is to pay genuine claims promptly and efficiently. The claim function exists to fulfil the takaful fund's promise to its participants by the takaful operator. The operator's reputation for settling claims has a direct impact on its ability to attract new participants and retain existing ones.

Settlement of Claims

Every takaful operator develops a process for handling claims. This process must consider which events are covered and which are excluded (not covered).

Events Covered

A claim can only be paid if the loss is covered. A takaful PMD clearly states which events are covered; these may include death, disability or car theft, among others. When the takaful operator's claims department receives claim intimation, the department checks whether the loss is among the covered events. If it is, they proceed further.

List of Exclusions

A takaful PMD contains a list of exclusions, which sets out the events that are not covered. For example, the list may include self-inflicted injuries or losses that occur while the participant is committing a crime. The claims department must check whether or not the intimated loss is included in the list of exclusions.

Process of Settling Claims

The process of settling claims may vary, but in general it follows these steps.

Step 1: The Participant or Nominee Intimates the Claim

When a loss occurs, the participant or beneficiary (also called the nominee) must report it to the takaful operator immediately. Any delay could result in evidence being lost, which could hamper the process of determining the claim and the proximate cause of loss. For example, let's suppose that a fire breaks out in a building during an earthquake. The owner of the building has takaful cover against fire only, but the proximate cause of the fire seems to be the earthquake. Therefore, evidence is needed to assess whether the claim should be paid. Similarly, in most family takaful policies, there is an initial 13-month period during which death due to suicide is not covered. If a claim is intimated late, it may be problematic to determine the exact cause of a death that seems to be the result of suicide.

Step 2: The Claim Is Recorded

It is important for takaful operators to record claims in their books when they are received. This ensures that the operator's accounts reflect the operator's true financial position, with up-to-date details of its liabilities. The principle of prudence also requires that liabilities are recorded immediately, while receivables are recorded once they have been confirmed.

Step 3: Claim Forms Are Issued

After receiving a claim intimation, the takaful operator issues claim forms in order to collect the information needed and find out about the circumstances leading up to the covered event. The information is collected in order to determine the following.

- *Cause of Loss*

  The takaful operator checks whether the cause of loss is covered. For example, if the cover is limited to a participant's accidental death, their natural death is not covered. In such a case, claim forms are not usually issued at all. However, if death due to any cause is covered and the participant also has ADB cover, it is important to find out the exact cause of death in order to decide on the claim for accidental death as well.
- *Extent of Loss*

  In general takaful, information about the extent of loss is provided by the participant in the claim form. For example, if a covered vehicle has been in an accident and is partially damaged, it is important to know what the extent of the damage is in order to process the claim.

Step 4: The Claim Is Investigated, If Necessary
Takaful companies have the right to investigate a claim to find out if it is genuine in relation to factors such as the cause of death and the extent of the loss. In the proposal form, there is always a declaration signed by the participant allowing the company to investigate their claim by checking the relevant records and so on.

When a large sum is assured in family takaful, natural deaths occurring within two years of the cover commencing are usually investigated by the takaful operator's claims department in order to avoid the operator paying fraudulent claims. The claim investigator also attempts to find out whether the participant concealed any information or made a material misstatement (e.g., concealing important information to keep the contribution rate low) when they took out the cover, which would violate the principle of utmost good faith. Any misrepresentation is considered material if the underwriter might have changed their decision if they had known the true situation.

Usually, in general takaful claims, only a third-party claim surveyor or loss adjuster licensed by the regulatory authority is allowed to investigate and process claims. Claims made under general takaful are more difficult to settle than claims made under family takaful for the following reasons.

- In life claims, there is no need to ascertain the extent of loss, because the sum assured (along with any profit from investing contributions) has to be paid to the beneficiary when the participant dies. However, in general takaful (e.g., claims relating to a car accident, a fire or goods damaged in transit), the extent of the loss does need to be determined.
- Finding out the exact cause of loss is also more complex in general takaful than it is for life claims.
- To avoid disputes between takaful operators and participants about general takaful claims, an independent claim surveyor or loss adjuster is engaged in the process. This ensures that a more impartial approach is taken to settling claims. Understanding the role of the surveyor is important, so we will discuss this in detail later in this chapter.

Step 5: The Claim Is Processed
In family takaful, the beneficiary (nominee)—or, in general takaful, the participant—completes the claim documents and sends them to the takaful operator for processing. In this section, we will focus on how the claim

is processed in family takaful. We will look at how it is processed in general takaful later in this chapter.

Death claim documents contain the following information.

- *Date of Death*
  The date of death is important because the takaful operator's claims department needs to check whether the participant's cover was in force (active) at the time when they died.
- *Cause of Death*
  The claims department also needs to check whether or not the cause of death is covered. For example, death due to suicide is not usually covered in the first 13 months of cover. There can be other exclusions as well. If the cause was an accident, the operator also needs to check whether the participant had accidental death benefit. Death caused by terrorism is not treated as accidental death, so this also needs to be checked. If the participant died of natural causes, the takaful operator needs to contact their doctor to ask questions about the participant's health and the cause of their death.
- *The Beneficiary's Identification*
  A person arranges family takaful so that if they die, their nominee (e.g., their widow, widower, children or parents) receives some compensation. For this purpose, the participant appoints a beneficiary who will receive the compensation. Therefore, it is extremely important that the takaful operator's claims department confirms the identity of the beneficiary who is making a claim.

Step 6: The Claim Is Approved

Once all the death claim documents (including death certificate, claim forms) have been checked, any investigations have been completed, the takaful company is convinced that the participant died on the dates provided and the beneficiary's identity has been confirmed, then a claims committee usually approves the admission (approval) of the claim and the beneficiary is informed. The beneficiary is also asked to provide their bank account details. A discharge certificate is also taken from the beneficiary (nominee) that frees the company from all future claims in the particular membership.

Step 7: The Claim Is Paid

When the claims department receives the beneficiary's bank account details, the payment is made to the beneficiary.

Case Studies 11.1 and 11.2 illustrate how the process of settling family takaful claims works in practice.

Case Study 11.1 Claims Calculation in Unit-Linked Plan

Mr Shams approaches a takaful company to arrange a unit-linked cover. He fills an application form, providing the following information.

Gender: Male

Profession: Teacher

Monthly income: USD 20,000

Health: Medically fit; no family history of natural deaths before 55 years of age

Beneficiary: Mrs Shamim

Sum assured: USD 100,000

Duration of cover: 19 years

Commencement (risk) date: 1 January 2010

Supplementary benefits (riders): FIB at 20% for 19 years; AIB

The underwriter goes through the aforementioned information and asks Mr Shams to have a medical examination following a medical requirements chart similar to the one displayed in Exhibit 10.2. After looking at the findings of the medical examination, the underwriter puts Mr Shams into the standard risk class. The underwriter applies the contribution rate for standard risk and issues the requested cover in return for an annual contribution of USD 2800. On contributing this, Mr Shams becomes a participant of the takaful fund.

After contributing USD 2800 annually for three years, he dies in a road accident. Mrs Shamim, the beneficiary, informs the takaful operator about the death of her husband and explains that he was covered. After checking their records, the claims department sends death claim forms to Mrs Shamim. Meanwhile, the claims department calculates the payable amount and records it in its books of accounts and creates reserves for it in order to make the payment. The claim may be investigated if needed. The claims department makes the calculation as follows:

Last contribution paid: 1 January 2012

Date of death: 1 February 2012

(*continued*)

Case Study 11.1 (continued)

Cause of death: Road traffic accident

Cash value of units allocated in three years: USD 8000

Amount Payable in Death Claim

Sum assured: USD 100,000 (A)

AIB: USD 100,000 (B)

FIB at 20% to be paid in instalments over 16 years (the remaining term of the cover): (100,000 × 0.2 × 16) = USD 320,000 (C)

Cash value of units allocated: USD 8000

Total: (A + B + C) = USD 528,000.

Case Study 11.2 Death Claim Calculation in Unit-Linked Takaful Plan

Mr Ethan asks for family takaful cover and provides the following information in an application form.

Gender: Male

Profession: Computer operator

Monthly income: USD 15,000

Health: Medically fit; no family history of natural deaths before 60 years of age (the given age may vary from company to company)

Beneficiary: Mrs Saansa

Required cover (sum assured): USD 500,000

Duration of cover: 15 years

The underwriter goes through the aforementioned information given by Ethan in the proposal form and asks for proof of any additional income and tax payments, as the amount of cover he requested (the sum assured) does not match his monthly income. (There is a risk of moral hazard if the desired cover is not justified by the applicant's income.) To exclude moral hazard, the underwriter asks client for proof of additional income. He provides property documents showing the amount of rent he has received along with tax documents showing the tax he has paid to the relevant authorities. He also provides evidence of additional income from his property, which is around USD 8000 per month. After looking at the results of Ethan's medical examination, the underwriter treats him as a standard risk, applies the

(*continued*)

Case Study 11.2 (continued)

contribution rate for standard risk and issues the cover in return for an annual contribution of USD 30,000. After contributing USD 30,000 into takaful fund, Mr B becomes a participant of the takaful fund.

After paying contributions for five years, Ethan dies of a heart attack. Saansa—his widow and the beneficiary—informs the company of her husband's death and explains that he was covered with the takaful operator. After checking the records, the claims department sends her the claim forms. Meanwhile, the claims department calculates the death claim, records it in its books and creates reserves for paying it. The payment is calculated as follows:

Last contribution paid: 1 January 2014

Supplementary contracts (riders) attached:

FIB at 20% for 15 years

Date of death: 1 June 2014

Cause of death: Heart attack

Cash value of units allocated in five years: USD 30,000

Amount Payable in Death Claim

Sum covered/assured: USD 500,000 (A)

FIB at 20% to be paid in instalments over 10 years (the remaining term of the cover): (500,000 × 0.2 × 10) = USD 1 million (B)

Cash value of units allocated: USD 30,000 (C)

Total: (A + B + C) = USD 1,530,000.

Case Study 11.3 Calculation of Contribution and Claims in Unit-Linked Family Takaful Plan

Mr Ali takes unit-linked family takaful with following particulars:

Face value/sum assured: USD 1,000,000

Age: 30 years

Duration/term: 20 years

Profession: Police officer

Annual contribution = 77,000

Commencement date = Risk date = 01.01.2014

Sum covered formula (For PTF) = face value − cash value (PIF)

Also shown is the breakup of how annual contribution is allocated between participant investment account (PIA) and participant taka-

(*continued*)

Case Study 11.3 (continued)

ful fund (PTF), also called waqf fund, and from PTF to share holder fund (SHF) considering the higher proportion of commission to takaful consultant in the initial years. Calculation of death claim if the client dies in the first or third year and the maturity value if participant survives the term of the plan is also shown.

Breakup of Contribution:

a) **Basic coverage**

Normal rate of takaful contribution/donation
At age 30: USD 1.5 per 1000
At age 31: USD 1.6 per 1000
At age 32: USD 1.7 per 1000
Added risk/Occupational extra: +0.2 per 1000
After adjusting risk:
At age 30: USD 1.5 per 1000
At age 31: USD 1.6 per 1000
At age 32: USD 1.7 per 1000

b) **Riders/supplementary contracts**

FIB: 15% for 20 years
Rate = 1.5 per 1000 (normal), 1.7 per 1000 (risk adjusted)
AD&D: 0.4 per 1000 (normal), 0.6 per 1000 (risk adjusted)
Basic coverage: 1700
FIB: 5100
AD&D: 600
Total premium: 77,000

1. **First-year contribution split:**

Agent fee (wakalah fee):
SHF = @ 60% = 46,200
PIA = 30,800
PTF = 7400 (for simplifying calculation charged annually. In actual it is charged monthly resulting in higher amount for investment)
PIA residue = 23,400
Total = 77,000

(continued)

Case Study 11.3 (continued)

Total riders: 5100 + 600 + basic 1700 goes to PTF/waqf fund

Total wakalah fee to be charged from PTF @25% = 1850

Total charges (agent fee + PTF) = 48,050 (46,500@ 60% + 1850 needed by company for its other expenses + profit margin for SHF)

Commission in individual family takaful unit-linked plan is almost 50% of the total contribution: (77,000) (0.5) = 38,500

Amount going to SHF: 48,050

Suppose unit price is 200 so total units purchased with amount USD 38,500 is:

192.50 (units in PIA)

Total number of units to be purchased = total investment amount/ unit price = 38,500/200 = 192.5,

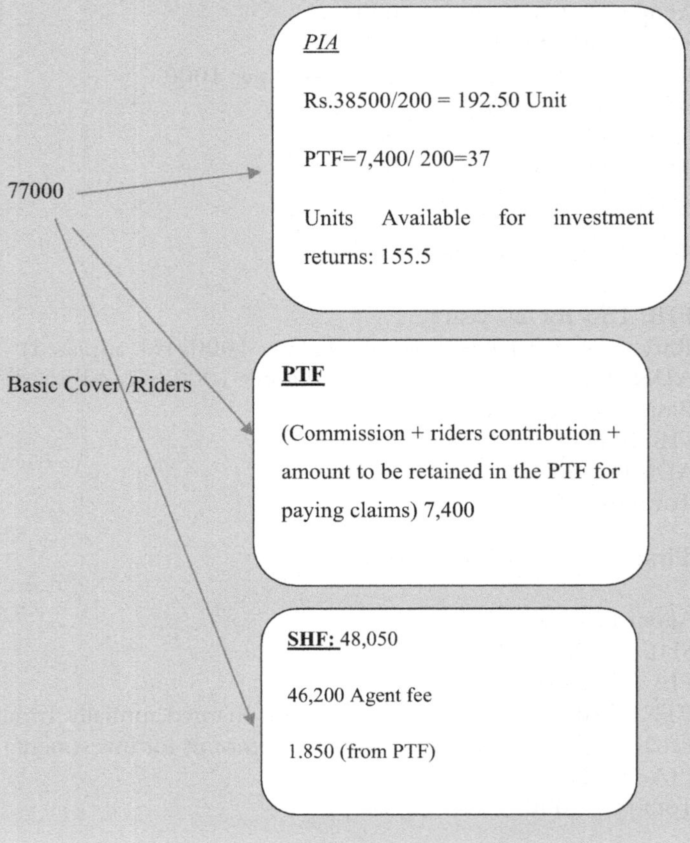

(*continued*)

Case Study 11.3 (continued)

Second-year contribution due date 01.01. 2015:

Age now is 31 years, rates for basic and FIB will change

On 01.01.2015, unit rate is USD 250/-

Suppose wakalah fee for second-year commission is 32% of annual contribution = 24,640

out of which 25% of contribution is for commission = 19,250

Amount to be retained in PTF = 7460 (5730 riders contribution and 1730 for claim against basic contribution)

PIF = already available = 38,875 (155.5 × 250)

PIF = new units purchased = 52,360 (209.44 units@250)

Total PIF = 91,235

Less: PTF = 7460

PIF residue = 83,775

SHF

@ 32% = 24,640

+ 25% of PTF = 7,460 × 0.25 = 1,865

Total SHF = 26,505

Total number of units available for investment = total investment amount/unit price = 83,775/250 = 335.10

Third-year contribution due date 01.01. 2016:

Age now is 32 years, rates for basic and FIB will change

On 01.01.2016, unit rate is USD 300

Suppose agent fee for third-year commission is 15% of annual contribution = 11,550 which is for commission

Amount to be retained in PTF = 7,314.64 (5730 riders contribution and 1584.64 for claim against basic contribution)

PIF = already available = 100,529 (335.1 × 300)

PIF = new units purchased = 65,450(518.1667 units@300)

Total PIF = 165,979.97

Less: PTF = 7,314.64

PIF residue = 158,665.33

SHF

@ 15% = 11,550

+ 25% of PTF = 7314.64 × 0.25 = 1828.66

Total SHF = 13,378.66

(continued)

Case Study 11.3 (continued)

Total number of units available for investment = total investment amount/unit price = 158,665.33/300 = 528.88

Death claim calculation if death occurs in the first year

Commencement date = risk date = 01.01.2014
Date of death (DOD) = 01.09.2014
Cause of death: road traffic accident (RTA)
Unit price on DOD = USD 245
Cash value of units = 245 × 155.5 = 38,097.50
Payable claim = face value + FIB + AD&D

Face value = USD 1,000,000 (961,902.50 to be paid from PTF and 38,097.50 from PIF under the basic coverage)

FIB is payable for 19 years and 03 months = 150,000 × 19
= 2,850,000 + 37500
= 2,887,500/-
AD&D = 1000,000
Payable claim = face value + FIB + AD&D
= 1,000,000 + 2,887,500 + 1,000,000
= 4,887,500/-

Death claim calculation if death occurs in the third year

Commencement date = risk date = 01.01.2014
Date of death (DOD) = 01.09.2016
Cause of death road traffic accident (RTA)
Unit price on DOD = USD 385
Accumulated units = 528.88
Cash value of units = 528.88 × 385 = 203,620.51
Payable claim = face value + FIB + AD&D

Face value = USD 1000,000 (796,379.49 to be paid from PTF and 203,620.51 from PIF under the basic coverage)

FIB is payable for 17 years and 03 months = 150,000 × 17
= 2,550,000 + 37500
= 2,587,500
AD&D = 1,000,000
Payable claim = face value + FIB + AD&D
= 1000,000 + 2,587,500 + 1,000,000
= 4,587,500

<u>On maturity</u>

Cash value in PIF = total accumulated units × unit price

Examples of death claim forms are displayed: in Exhibit 11.1, claimant form; in Exhibit 11.2, employer form and in Exhibit 11.3, physician statement form.

Pak-Qatar Family Takaful Ltd.
102-103, Business Arcade, PECHS Block 6
Shahrah E Faisal,
Karachi
021-111-825-238 (Ext 115)

Death Claim Form

CLAIMANT'S STATEMENT

Completion Instructions:

1. This form may be completed by those having a claim for death benefits as a person nominated by the participant, Guardian, Assignee, Trustee or a successor
2. Separate forms will be required for each claimant if more than one. However only one form is required for all memberships where the deceased was covered.
3. Please complete the form with legible handwriting, incomplete form may cause delay in processing of death benefits.
4. This form should be duly attested by notary public, Nazim of a union council or above, executive of Pak-Qatar Family Takaful Limited or class 1 officer of the federal/provincial government.
5. Copies wherever referred below means certified true copies. Documents issued/prepared in any language other than Urdu or English will be accepted only when accompanied by a certified translation in Urdu/English.

MEMBERSHIP NUMBER(S):			
AMOUNT CLAIMED:			

CLAIMANT'S INFORMATION

Last Name:	First Name:	Middle Name:	❑ Mr. ❑ Mrs.	❑ Miss ❑ Ms.	Marital status (circle one) Single / Married/ Divorcee /Widow
Father/Husband's Name:	Relationship With deceased:	Birth date: DD/MM /YYYY	Gender: ❑ M ❑ F		
Street address: City:		Phone no.: ( )			
Correspondence address:	City:	Cell No: ( )			
CNIC NO:	Email address:				
Bank Branch:	Bank Account Number:	Banker's Name:			
Claiming the benefit as:	❑ Nominee ❑ Guardian ❑ Successor ❑ Assignee ❑ other (Specify)				
Name(s) of other legal heirs of the deceased with relationship and age(s) :					

Exhibit 11.1 Claimant form

INFORMATION ABOUT THE DECEASED

Last Name:	First Name:	Middle Name:	Birth date: DD /MM /YYYY	Gender: ❑ M ❑ F	Date of Death: DD /MM /YYYY

Cause of Death:	Duration of Illness: From: To:
Briefly describe the circumstances leading to death:	

Father/Husband's Name:	CNIC NO:	Place of Death:

Occupation:	Employer:	Deceased's Last Working day: DD /MM /YYYY
Employer address:		Employer phone no.: ( )

Was the deceased covered by Takaful/insurance from any other company?	❑ Yes ❑ No (If the answer is Yes pl. provide detail below)

Number of Membership/Policy: 1. 2. 3.	Date of Issue:	Company's Name and Address :

Date when the deceased complained about his illness: DD /MM /YYYY	What was the complaint about?

Detail of all treatments taken immediately prior to death:

Doctor/ Hospital Name	Address	Complaint/Illness	Date of treatment:
1.			
2.			
3.			

Exhibit 11.1 (continued)

Detail of all treatments taken in previous three years:			
Doctor/ Hospital Name 1. 2. 3.	Address	Complaint/Illness	Date of treatment:

Please attach a certified copy of the original of the following documents–if available/applicable:

— Participant Membership document	☐ attached
— Death certificate (burial certificate if buried abroad)	☐ attached
— Assignment letter	☐ attached
— Copy of CNIC (deceased)	☐ attached
— Copy of passport of deceased (if deceased living abroad)	☐ attached
— Copy of CNIC (claimant)	☐ attached
— Copy of passport of claimant (if claimant living abroad)	☐ attached
— Copies of police report, post mortem report, newspaper clipping (in case of accidental/unnatural death)	☐ attached
— Others:____	☐ attached
	☐ attached

DECLARATION

I hereby declare that the answers to all the questions were entered completely and truthfully and nothing has been concealed or misrepresented.

I hereby authorize Pak-Qatar Family Takaful Ltd.

1. Knowing that the authorization will be used in determining the eligibility of the payment of death benefit in this(ese) contracts and will be used for processing of these benefits only;
2. To require and collect medical and non medical information regarding the deceased from all hospitals/doctors, medical facilities, federal, provincial and local government agencies, law enforcement agencies, Federal Bureau of Revenue, NADRA, Banks, takaful, insurance Retakaful and reinsurance companies and request all of them to provide all such information pertaining to the deceased;
3. And the deceased had during his life time authorized the company to have access to such information pertaining him.

Signature of Claimant	Name of Attestor
Date	*Address*

I hereby declare that the information set forth herein is true to the best of my knowledge and belief.

Signature of the Attestor: Year Month Day

Exhibit 11.1 (continued)

FAMILY TAKAFUL

Pak-Qatar Family Takaful Limited

Form D-1

Employer's Statement

Note :
Please don't leave any blank, unanswered question, date and/or signature, wherever applicable

1. Policy holder's information

Name of Company

Takaful Policy No. | Policy Start Date

2. Participant's information

a. Deceased' Name:

b. Father's Name/Husband's Name:

c. Date of Birth of deceased: Age : NIC No.

d. Residentional Address:

Contact No.

e. Proof of age: ☐ National Identity Card ☐ Metric Certificate ☐ Other (Please specify)

3. Occupational Information

a. Employee No.

b. Date of Joining of Company

c. Designation

d. Annual Salary

e. Occupation (at date of Death)

4. Event Information

a. Date of Diagnosis

b. Date of Death

c. Place of Death

d. Primary Cause of Death

e. Secondary cause

f. On what date did deceased last attend his usual work?

g. When did deceased first complain of or give other indications of his/her last illness?

h. When did deceased last complain or consulted of his/her last illness?

5. Claim Information

a. Amount of Claim

b. Title of Cheque

8. Decleration by Employer/Authorized representative

The undersigned, hereby makes claim to said Takaful coverage and hereby agrees that the written statement s and affidavits of all the physicians who attended to or treated the Participant shall constitute and they are hereby made a part of these proofs of death and further agrees that the furnishing of this form, or of any nor a waiver of any of its right or defenses.

Furthermore, I/We hereby authorize, any physicians, hospitals, clinic or medical service provider, insurance company, or any other institution, or any person, who has any record or information about above mentioned life to provide Pak-Qatar Family Takaful Limited complete information including copies of records with reference to any sickness, accident, disability treatment , examination, medical investigation , advise or hospitalization underwent. A photocopy of this authorization shall be as valid as the original.

Claimant Signature:

Name:

Date:

Company Stamp

Checklist

☐ Form D-2 Physician's statement

☐ Copy of CNIC

☐ Copy of Death Certificate (hospital)

☐ Copy of Burial Certificate (Municipal Town)

☐ Copy of FIR (*in case of Accidental Death*)

☐ Copy of Autopsy report (*in case of Accidental Death*)

Please ensure to enclosed above mentioned document in order to avoid any delay

Ref No.: GT/CL/2008/00051/1

Please return to :
Customer Services Department
Pak-Qatar Family Takaful Limited
Suite # 203, 2nd Floor, Business Arcade, Plot No 27/A, Block 6,P.E.C.H.S., Karachi, Pakistan

Exhibit 11.2 Employer form

FAMILY TAKAFUL

Pak-Qatar Family Takaful Limited Form D-2

Physician's Statement

Note :
All answer must be in Physician's handwrting
Please don't leave any blank, unanswered question, date and/or signature, wherever applicable

1.Deceasd's information

a. Deceased' Name:

b. Father's Name/Husband's Name:

c. Date of Birth of deceased: Age : NIC No.

d. Residential Address:

Contact No.

2. Event Information

a. Date of Death

b. Place of Death

If died in hospital or other medical institution, please give name

c. Primary Cause of Death

d. Secondary Cause of Death

e. Interval between onset and death

From	To	No of Days

3. Past medical history

a. When did deceased first complain of or give other indications of his/her last illness?

b. Date last consulted or took medical advise of his/her last illness?

c. Have you treated or advised any treatment prior to last illness? ☐ Yes ☐ No

d. Did the deceased, to your knowledge, receive treatment during the last five year from any other physician, or hospital? ☐ Yes ☐ No

Date	Physician/hospital Name	Nature of Illness	Treatment

4. Accidental Death/Suicide, homicide

a. Cause of death, please specify ☐ Accident ☐ Suicide ☐ Homicide ☐ Other

b. Please describe event in detail

c. Was an inquest/investigation held? ☐ Yes ☐ No

d. Was an autopsy performed ☐ Yes ☐ No if yes, please describe findings in detail

if yes, please describe findings

5.Decleration

I hereby declared that to the best of my knowledge and belief the information given herein is true and complete

Signature:

Name: Contact No.

Date of statement:

Stamp

Please return to :

Customer Services Department

Pak-Qatar Family Takaful Limited
Suite # 203, 2nd Floor, Business Arcade, Plot No 27/A, Block 6,P.E.C.H.S., Karachi, Pakistan

Ref No.: GT/CL/2008/00052/1

Exhibit 11.3 Physician statement form

Objectives of the Claim Function

Paying claims is the litmus test for any takaful operator. Participants take out cover to protect themselves and their families if they get into financial trouble because of an unfortunate event. They contribute into takaful fund with the expectation that they will be compensated if an event they are covered for occurs. Therefore, the task of the claims department is very delicate. On the one hand, it has to pay claims without delay; on the other hand, it has to avoid paying fraudulent or exaggerated claims.

The claims department has the following two main goals.

1. *To keep the contractual promises set out in the policy.*

A takaful operator keeps its promise by providing a prompt, fair and equal service to participants and their beneficiaries.

2. *To avoid paying fraudulent claims.*

The takaful operator should have an effective claims-settlement process to control costs and ensure that covered losses are reimbursed in a fair manner. Participants are entitled to a fair resolution of their claims. However, overcompensating participants for their claims will increase the contribution rate for all participants. Conversely, unpaid claims that are covered by the contract can result in angry participants, litigation and regulatory sanctions.

Sharing Information About Claims

To make better use of information, it is important for the claims department to share its findings and data with other departments in the takaful company: the marketing department, the underwriting department and the actuarial department.

Marketing Department

- The marketing department needs information about customer satisfaction. In addition, it can use information gathered by the claims department to develop new types of cover that better meet participants' needs.

- Staff in the claims department must inform the underwriting department about court rulings that affect the takaful operator's exposure to loss or its pricing, such as interpretations of policy exclusions or the application of limits.

Underwriting Department

- Evaluating the costs associated with claims made can reveal loss characteristics that an underwriter may have been able to detect when considering an application for insurance.
- Reviewing individual claims can uncover operations and activities that, if the underwriter had carried out more thorough investigations, might have led them to either refuse the application or offer the cover on a different basis. As a result, the company may refine their underwriting procedures and identify appropriate training for underwriters.
- Very close coordination is needed between a takaful operator's claims and underwriting departments. For example, data on causes of death gathered by the claims department can alert the underwriting department to new trends, which can help refine the underwriting process.

Actuarial Department

- Employees in the actuarial department require accurate information about the real cost of claims. They also need up-to-date information on claims that have occurred.
- Data on causes of death collected by the claims department can help the actuarial department revise their additional contribution rate for clients who bring a higher than average risk to the fund, based on emerging health trends and problems related to particular professions.

The Claims Process and the Surveyor's Role in General Takaful

Almost all general takaful claims are processed by licensed surveyors.

In general takaful, when a loss occurs, the participant reports it to the takaful operator. Up to a specified amount (which is always small), the takaful operator can process the claim in-house. However, when that limit is exceeded, every takaful operator is legally bound to refer such claims to a licensed surveyor.

Who Is the Surveyor?

A surveyor is a person who is technically competent in settling general takaful claims and is licensed by the regulator. A surveyor uses technical skills to:

- Establish the cause of loss or damage
- Assess the extent of the loss
- Provide a complete picture of the situation in a report

The claimant (the participant making the claim) has to:

- Prove that the loss or damage has occurred
- Prove that it occurred within the period covered by the policy
- Demonstrate that they had an interest in the goods at the time of loss

The surveyor assists in this process by collecting information and documents. When a participant reports a loss to the takaful operator, the takaful operator sends the claim, along with the participant's PMD, to the surveyor. The surveyor studies the details and checks whether the cause of the loss is covered. If the cause of the loss is covered, the surveyor assesses the extent of the loss and checks the amount that has been claimed by the participant.

The surveyor sends a report to the takaful operator stating (based on their expertise) whether the loss is covered and, if it is covered, the amount that should be payable to the participant.

Let's look at the surveyor's role in the context of two case studies.

Case Study 11.4 Motor Takaful Claim for a Private Vehicle

Mrs Sarah arranges comprehensive motor takaful cover for a car. Unfortunately, a few weeks later, the car is damaged. She reports the damage to takaful operator.

The operator asks her to take the car to a panel workshop. In the meantime, the operator sends the claim details and PMD to the surveyor. The surveyor checks the documents and decides that the claim is payable.

Next, the surveyor visits the workshop. The surveyor takes pictures of the damaged car and discusses the cost of repairing it with

(*continued*)

Case Study 11.4 (continued)

the workshop. After some negotiation with the workshop, the surveyor agrees to a cost for the full repair. The surveyor reports the outcome to the takaful operator.

Once the surveyor receives approval from the operator, the surveyor asks the workshop to repair the car. She pays the deprecation cost to the workshop, which sends a bill for the outstanding repair costs to the takaful operator.

The surveyor then issues a report to the takaful operator, which includes the following information.

- The details of claim, including details of the accident.
- Photos of the damaged car.
- Details of the settlement made with the workshop.
- Photos of the repaired car.
- Cash receipts.

Based on the report, the takaful operator settles the claim with Sarah.

Case Study 11.5 Motor Takaful Claim for a Commercial Vehicle

Person B is driving a company car, which meets with an accident in 2016. The vehicle is covered under a comprehensive commercial vehicle policy with a takaful company. Person B's employer makes a claim. The details of the cover and claim are as follows.

Type of vehicle: Commercial
Value: USD 100,000
Excess: USD 5000
Total claim: USD 30,000
Labour charges: USD 10,000
Value of new parts: USD 20,000
Year of manufacture: 2014
Age of vehicle: 2 years
Depreciation (10% per year for 2 years): 20%

(continued)

Case Study 11.5 (continued)

Scale of Depreciation Considering Useful Life of Vehicles as 10 Years

S. no	*Age of the vehicle*	*Scale of depreciation (%)*
1	0–6 months	05
2	More than 6 months and up to 12 months	10
3	More than 12 months and up to 24 months	20
4	More than 24 months and up to 36 months	30
5	More than 36 months and up to 48 months	40
6	More than 48 months and up to 60 months	50
7	More than 60 months and up to 72 months	60

Total Amount Payable by Person B's Employer

Depreciation on new parts: (20% × USD 20,000) = USD 4000

Total Claim Payable to Person B's Employer

Labour charges, plus value of new parts (less depreciation), less excess:

(USD 10,000 + USD 20,000 – USD 4,000 – USD 5000) = USD 21,000.

Pak-Qatar General Takaful Limited

GENERAL TAKAFUL

Suite # 402-404
Business Arcade
Block 6, Sharea Faisal
P.E.C.H.S.,
Karachi.

Contact Details:
Phone (92 21) 34380357-61
Fax No. (92 21) 34386453
Email info@pakqatar.com.pk
Web: www.pakqatar.com.pk

MOTOR VEHICLE NOTICE OF ACCIDENT FORM

THIS FORM MUST BE RETURNED TO THE COMPANY IMMEDIATELY WITH ALL QUESTIONS FULLY ANSWERED WHETHER A CLAIM IS LIKELY TO ARISE OR NOT

The Company does not admit liability by issue of this form

Please read this form thoroughly before filling in details

PARTICIPANT

Name ______

Occupation ______

Address ______

______ Telephone No. ______

PARTICULARS OF VEHICLE CONCERNED IN ACCIDENT

Policy No. ______ Expiry Date ______

Make, year and Cost Price	Horse Power	Registered Letters and Numbers	For what purpose was the vehicle being used? For what purpose generally used?

Was a Trailer attached? ______
How many persons were in the vehicle at the time? ______
Is policy-holder the owner of the vehicle? ______
Was the vehicle being used with the owner's knowledge and consent? ______

If Motorcycle
(1) Was a sidecar attached ______
(2) Was a Pillion Rider carried? ______

If "Goods Carrying" Vehicle:
(1) State nature and approximate weight of load carried? ______
(2) Was a Trailer attached? ______

Exhibit 11.4 Motor accident claim form

DRIVER	Name of the Driver at the time of Accident__________ Age ______ Address of Driver__________ Is the driver { Owner? __________ / Owner's Regular paid Driver? __________ / Owner's Relative or Friend? __________ Licence No. ______ Date of Issue ______ Date of Expiry ______ Has it been endorsed? If so, give particulars __________ Has the driver previously been involved in an accident? __________ If Paid Driver, how long has he been in your employment? __________ Was the driver under the influence of alcohol or drug at the time of the accident? ______ State exactly what alcohol or drink or drugs the driver had in the 8 hours immediately preceding the accident and where { __________
STATE HOW ACCIDENT, LOSS OR BREAKDOWN OCCURRED	Date ______ Time______ Place ______ Estimated speed of your vehicle______km per hour ______ How did you signal your approach? __________ Give full description of accident, loss, breakdown: __________
WITNESSES It is most important that Names and Addresses of all independent witnesses of accident should be obtained, whether the driver considers himself to blame or not	Give names and addresses of all Witnesses of Accident: Passengers in car { __________ Independent Witnesses: { __________ If witness names not taken give reason __________ Did a Police Sepoy witness the accident or take particulars?__________ Sepoy's No. __________ Was any statement, as to fault, made by the witness or driver at the time? ______ Was the matter reported to the police? If so, give the name and address of the Police Station and state what action, if any has or is being taken? __________

Exhibit 11.4 (continued)

PARTICULARS OF DAMAGE OR INJURY TO THIRD PARTY (PROPERTY OR PERSON)	Name : ______ Address : ______ Full extent of Personal Injuries or Damage to Property ______ If any injured person has been moved to hospital or medically attended, give the name and address of the hospital or doctor ______ Has notice of any claim been given to you? ______ Admit no liability in any circumstances but despatch to the Company forewith and unanswered any written communication which may have been received.
PARTICULARS OF DAMAGE TO INSURED VEHICLE	Full particulars of damage______ Estimated cost of repairs ______ Address where damaged vehicle may be inspected ______ Have you given any instruction as to repairs being started and if so, to whom?______ Have you instructed them to send an estimate to the company immediately?______ In the event of damage to tyre as a result of the Accident state: Make ______ Size ______Type ______ When purchased ______ Approximate Mileage done ______ Has it been rethreaded? ______ When ______
THEFT	ALSO TO BE FILLED, IN CASE OF THEFT (1) If loss occurred while the vehicle was standing in the street, was it unattended. If so, how long? (2) If car was in the garage, was forcible entry made, if so, in what manner?______ (3) Have the police been advised? If so, and with what result? (4) Was any damage inflicted to the car? (5) Is a paid driver kept? If so, how long has he been in your employment? (6) Please state any further particulars

Exhibit 11.4 (continued)

SKETCH	Please make a rough plan of the road in the space reserved below illustrating the position of vehicle and person concerned at the time of the accident. An arrow should indicate the directions in which they were moving.

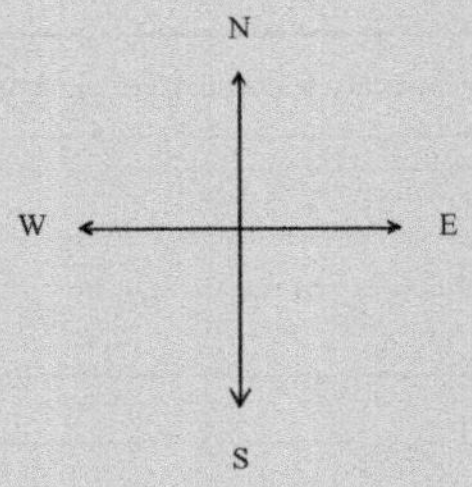

Is there any other policy indemnifying you or the driver of this accident?

I / We hereby declare the foregoing particulars to be true in every respect and claim under the policy.

The amount of my / our loss

Date : ______________________ Participant Signature: ______________________

Exhibit 11.4 (continued)

GENERAL TAKAFUL

Pak-Qatar General Takaful Limited

Suite # 402-404
Business Arcade
Block 6, Sharea Faisal
P.E.C.H.S.,
Karachi

Contact Details:
Phone (92 21) 34380357-61
Fax No. (92 21) 34386453
Email: info@pakqatar.com.pk
Web: www.pakqatar.com.pk

FIRE CLAIM FORM

Name of Claimant:		
Name of Participant:		
Policy No:	**Agency:**	
When did the Fire take place? Give Date & Time		
Situation of Property damaged or destroyed		
How were the premises occupied at date of Fire?		
What was the cause of the Fire, and under what circumstances did it occur?		
Does the policy give a correct description of the property in all respects as it existed immediately before the Fire?		
Has any element of risk been introduced which was not allowed by the policy?		
Have the conditions of the Policy been complied with in every respect?		
Is the Claimant the sole owner of the property damaged or destroyed? If not, state full particulars of any other interest.		
Has there been a previous Fire in these premises, or in any other premises in which the Insured was interested? If so, state full particulars, including the cause, of such Fire or Fires.		
Were there at the time of the Fire any other Takaful / Insurances, whether effected by the Claimant or any other person, on the said property, with any other Company or Society? If so, state full particulars. If not, please write "No"	**NAME OF COMPANY**	**AMOUNT**

I/We ____ of ______________________

do hereby declare that the abvoe is a full, true and acurate statement, and I / we further declare that the Articles mentioned on the other side, being my / our property, and participant under the above-named policy or policies, were accidentally destroyed or damaged, without any design or procurement on my / our part, by the aforesaid Fire/Peril according to the extent and values annexed; wherefore I/we claim from ________________ the sum of Rs.______________ the value thereof.

As witness my/our hand, this ______day of ________________ 200

Signature of Claimant ______________________________

Exhibit 11.5 Fire claim form

Chapter Summary

A test for any takaful operator is how it handles claims when an event covered occurs. A thorough analysis of the claim is necessary in order to differentiate between genuine and fraudulent claims. The operator is responsible for refusing fraudulent claims and processing genuine claims swiftly. The first steps in the process of handling claims are as follows.

- Intimation by the participant or nominee
- Recording claims in the operator's books
- Issuing claim forms

After receiving claim intimation, the operator issues claim forms in order to establish the following.

- Cause of loss: this should match the events covered; otherwise, the claim is not payable.
- Extent of loss: this usually applies in general takaful claims.
- Whether an investigation of the claim is needed.

General takaful claims are usually processed by licensed surveyors. Surveyors engage experts to assess losses relating to vehicles, buildings and machinery. Surveyors assist the takaful operator to decide whether or not the claim is payable and, if it is, the genuine amount to be paid.

CHAPTER 12

Regulating and Supervising Takaful

Abstract Takaful companies invite participants from public to deposit money into a takaful fund and become participants. For better safe-keeping of this money and more effective delivery of the services promised, proper regulation is a must. The regulator should develop a mechanism in which only sound individuals can establish takaful operators. The regulator should provide a licence only when it is satisfied with the expertise and transparency of the takaful operator's shareholders and its team. Takaful companies claim Shariah compliance; therefore, this claim should be checked by independent Shariah professionals. The role of Shariah professionals within the takaful operator is very important, as they perform important functions such as vetting products for Shariah compliance, approving investments from a Shariah point of view, refunding any surplus to participants and putting any doubtful profits into a charity fund.

Keywords Regulating • Takaful • Supervising takaful

After reading this chapter, you should understand:

- The main regulatory requirements for takaful operators
- The procedures required at company level for Shariah compliance
- The role of the Shariah advisor

A. Malik, K. Ullah, *Introduction to Takaful*,
https://doi.org/10.1007/978-981-32-9016-7_12

Introduction

Takaful operators invite participants of the public to join their takaful fund and get the takaful cover they need by depositing money in the form of contributions. By agreeing to provide cover to a participant, the takaful operator is promising to pay that participant compensation from the takaful fund if any of the events the participant is covered for occur. Such a promise should only be given by a sound entity with the necessary technical expertise and financial strength. Ensuring that a takaful company has these attributes is the responsibility of a regulator. An effective system of regulation, supervision and governance is needed within takaful operators and at the regulatory level.

In this chapter, we will discuss the rules and regulations that need to be in place to safeguard the interests of the participants and the shareholders.

Compliance by Takaful Operators

Governance of takaful companies is ensured by putting in place rules and regulation at two levels: regulatory and within a takaful operator.

Compliance at the Regulatory Level

In most countries, takaful and insurance companies are governed by the same regulator. A takaful operator has to comply with the rules for takaful companies in addition to the requirements applied to insurance companies. If there is a conflict between the two sets of rules, takaful operators should follow the rules for takaful companies.

Procedures Applied to Both Takaful and Insurance Companies

The regulator sets out the rules and procedures that are applied to takaful and insurance companies. We will look at some of these in this chapter.

Initially, a takaful or insurance company needs to be registered by law. Once it has been registered, it becomes a separate legal entity and may apply to the regulator for a licence to begin operating. The regulator may set the following conditions for issuing a licence to insurance or a takaful company.

1. *A Minimum Level of Capital*

Establishing any company requires capital. To protect the interests of customers, the regulator allows only sound companies to operate. Therefore, it requires them to raise a minimum level of capital. The regulator decides on the level of capital that a takaful or insurance company needs to have in order to begin operating in a sound manner.

- Paid-up capital is the amount of capital that a company actually issues and has received payment from the sale of its shares.
- Authorised capital is the maximum amount of capital that a company (or bank) can raise by selling its shares.
- Paid-up capital can be less than or equal to a company's authorised capital, but it can never exceed it.

2. *A Minimum Deposit*

Companies have to deposit (and keep deposited) a minimum amount in cash or approved securities with the regulator or a central bank. This is always a set amount or a percentage of the paid-up capital. In Pakistan, the deposit is 10% of the company's paid-up value. Companies can place any Shariah-compliant security, such as sukuks (Islamic bonds), with the central bank.

3. *An Actuary*

To calculate premiums and contributions in life insurance and family takaful companies, the companies must appoint an actuary.

4. *Vetting and Approval of Products*

Products developed by the company have to be vetted and approved by the regulator.

5. *Board of Directors*

The company must appoint board of directors, which must be composed in line with the regulator's requirements.

6. *Reinsurance or Re-takaful*

The company may need to arrange proper reinsurance or re-takaful containing the following details.

- The type of re-takaful (reinsurance) contract.
- The operator's maximum retention (the maximum amount of cover that a company can provide (retain) to a single client).
- The maximum liabilities under a total re-takaful treaty.
- An estimate of the total contributions a company expects to receive from its participants in a specified period.
- The names and addresses of re-takaful operators with their respective:
  - Shares and their ratings by reputable international rating agencies
  - Conduct of marketing staff
  - Nomination of beneficiaries
  - Licensing of surveyors
  - Minimum solvency levels.

Additional Responsibilities of the Regulator for Takaful Companies

Takaful companies claim Shariah compliance. Therefore, the regulator should put in place various procedures to ensure that this is the case. The regulator should establish a takaful division, which should have a central Shariah board that keeps a close check on the Shariah aspects of takaful operators.

The regulator may take following steps to ensure Shariah compliance in takaful operators.

1. *Vet the Products of Takaful Companies*

The regulator should vet takaful products in order to decide whether they comply with Shariah law.

2. *Assess Investment Policy*

Takaful companies claim that they invest the funds in Shariah-compliant opportunities. The regulator needs to confirm this.

3. *Set Criteria for Shariah Advisors*

The regulator should also decide the criteria for Shariah advisors and require every takaful operator to get approval from the regulator when appointing or removing a Shariah advisor.

4. *Takaful Model*

If a takaful operator has adopted a particular takaful model, for instance, wakalah model, then the regulator should frame with great care the procedures for determining the wakalah fee, making payments from the takaful fund and refunding any surplus.

5. *Determine the Wakalah Fee*

The regulator should decide the range of the wakalah fee for different types of takaful (such as family, health, motor, fire, marine and miscellaneous), keeping in mind the costs involved in bringing participants to the takaful fund for the respective type of takaful. The company's Shariah board or Shariah advisor may decide the wakalah fee within the range set by the regulator. A young takaful operator may set the wakalah fee at the higher end of the range; as time passes and the operator increases its membership, the operator should set the wakalah fee at the lower end of the range. In this way, the takaful fund grows and becomes stable.

6. *Participant Takaful Fund Policy*

Participants' claims are paid from the takaful fund; therefore, the regulator must ensure that only claims are paid from this fund and that it is never used for paying the takaful operator's administrative expenses. The profit of the shareholder (the takaful operator) may be linked to the generation of surplus for participants. Otherwise, the operator may be bringing excessive risk to the takaful fund while earning a wakalah fee. Such risks may result in abnormal cash outflow from the takaful fund. However, in a takaful operator's early years (e.g., the initial five years), a takaful company may be given exemption from this rule.

7. *Shariah Audit*

Usually, takaful operators establish an internal Shariah audit department and also arrange external Shariah audit. Regulator can also make it mandatory for both internal and external Shariah audit of the company. An external Shariah auditor should be approved by the regulator to conduct a Shariah audit. This audit will check takaful operators' claims that they are Shariah-compliant. The auditor will look at the following.

8. *Re-takaful Arrangements*

Takaful companies should arrange re-takaful instead of reinsurance. Reinsurance can be allowed only if the desired cover is not provided by re-takaful operators.

9. *Shariah-Compliance Systems at the Company Level*

Every takaful company should have a Shariah board, a full-time Shariah advisor and a Shariah-compliance team. The criteria for the Shariah advisor should be similar to the fit and proper criteria being followed by the State Bank of Pakistan for Islamic banks.

Procedures Required at the Operator Level for Shariah Compliance

Every takaful company should have a Shariah board, a full-time Shariah advisor and a Shariah-compliance team. The procedures framed by the regulator for Shariah compliance in takaful companies may include appointing:

- A Shariah supervisory board
- A full-time Shariah advisor
- A Shariah-compliance department, which may implement the directions and advice of the Shariah supervisory board and Shariah advisor

Shariah Board

The takaful operator may need to appoint a Shariah board with high-calibre participants who have knowledge of fiqh (the science of interpreting the Holy Quran and Sunnah), Islamic jurisprudence and modern financial dealings. The board may be given the responsibility of:

- Reviewing and approval of takaful products
- Ensuring Shariah compliance
- Approving it for sending to the regulator if the law requires

Because the takaful operator makes investments using the takaful fund, the Shariah board should establish procedures and rules to ensure that:

- Only those investments that are Shariah-compliant are allowed, so that participants are given permissible profits only.
- The practices of the takaful operator's employees conform to Islamic principles.
- Marketing staff adopt highly ethical practices for inviting potential participants to the takaful fund and convincing them to join. They should provide full information about the cover, any exclusions and the claim process.

The Shariah board should meet regularly, and the takaful operator should have systems in place to implement the board's procedures and rules for ensuring Shariah compliance. This may include appointing a full-time Shariah advisor and a Shariah-compliance department.

Full-Time Shariah Advisor

A takaful operator can appoint a Shariah advisor with the consent of the Shariah board and the approval of the regulator. If the management of the takaful operator is the only authority to decide on the appointment of a Shariah advisor, there is a risk that the operator will prefer to employ an advisor who will not object to the operator's products, investments and other operational practices.

A Shariah advisor is responsible for implementing the measures devised by the regulator and Shariah board for the operator's compliance. The Shariah advisor's responsibilities may include:

- Vetting products for Shariah compliance
- Approving investments from a Shariah point of view
- Refunding any surplus to participants
- Putting any doubtful profits into a charity fund

The Shariah advisor should report to the Shariah board.

By putting in place these systems, Shariah compliance in takaful companies can be effectively ensured.

Chapter Summary

Takaful companies invite participants of the public to deposit money into a takaful fund and become participants. For better safe-keeping of this money and more effective delivery of the services promised, proper regulation is a must. The regulator should develop a mechanism in which only sound individuals can establish takaful operators. The regulator should provide a licence only when it is satisfied with the expertise and transparency of the takaful operator's shareholders and its team.

Takaful companies claim Shariah compliance; therefore, this claim should be checked by independent Shariah professionals. The role of Shariah professionals within the takaful operator is very important, as they perform the following functions.

- Vetting products for Shariah compliance.
- Approving investments from a Shariah point of view.
- Refunding any surplus to participants.
- Putting any doubtful profits into a charity fund.

Glossary

Actuary A person who understands how insurance premiums and pension benefits are calculated and analyses the financial consequences of risk. They are the mathematicians of insurance companies.

Aqd mua'wza A contract of compensation; for example, a sale and purchase transaction.

Claim A formal request to an insurance or takaful company for a payment based on the terms of the contract.

Daman A guarantee.

Equitable premiums A premium is said to be equitable when it is determined based on the risk being transferred to the insurance company. (Also see 'Premium'.)

Fiqh The science of interpreting Quran and Sunnah

Gharar Excessive risk or danger (uncertainty) in transactions

Hadith A collection of the sayings of the Prophet (SAW) that Muslims follow as rulings.

Halal Shariah-permitted actions and things.

Haram Shariah-prohibited actions and things.

Kafala A guarantee.

Khathar Danger.

Maysir/Qimar Maysir and qimar are the extreme forms of gharar, where the participants in a transaction play a game of chance that can result in a large profit or loss.

A. Malik, K. Ullah, *Introduction to Takaful*,
https://doi.org/10.1007/978-981-32-9016-7

Model Any kind of simplification, substitute or stand-in for something that actually exists or that you are trying to predict.

Muamalat Dealings between people.

Mudarabah A capital and expertise partnership. One party contributes capital, and the other contributes expertise and action.

Mudarib The expert and working partner in a partnership contract.

Nasiah Paying more than the principal when taking out a loan due to the conditions of the loan.

Premium The amount paid by a client to an insurance company. It can also be called the price of the insurance.

Proximate cause The basic cause that triggers the chain of events resulting in damage.

Qard-e-hasna An interest-free loan recommended by Shariah.

Quran The Muslim holy book.

Rab ul maal The owner of capital in a partnership.

Re-takaful Takaful cover arranged by takaful companies for the better management of risk.

Riba A usury including conventional interest, which is considered unjust in Islam and other religions.

Riba al Hadith Excess compensation without any consideration resulting from the sale of specific goods.

Riba al Quran A conditional or understood increase versus a loan or debt.

Shariah Literally, *the way*. It is considered to be the revelation that Prophet Muhammad (SAW) received and practised; that is, the Quran and the Prophetic traditions.

Sum assured/sum covered The amount agreed by the insurance company and the client to be paid by the insurance company to the client if an insured event occurs.

Sunnah The sayings and deeds of Prophet Muhammad (SAW).

Surveyor (insurance/takaful) An insurance or takaful surveyor is a technically competent person who settles general claims and is licensed by the regulator.

Tabarru A donation or gift, the purpose of which is not commercial, but which seeks the pleasure of Allah. Any benefit that is given by one person to another without receiving anything in return is called tabarru.

Takaful A joint guarantee; the Islamic alternative to insurance.

Takaful operator A company that provides takaful.

Tareeq Way, passage or route.

Underwriting A process that a company employs to assess a potential client's eligibility for cover.

Usury In Shariah, usury means undue increase without any opposite consideration, which causes injustice in a financial transaction. (Also see 'Riba'.)

Wakalah Agency. In the context of takaful, it is when one party, usually the service organisation, assumes the role of agent to perform actions that benefit the other.

Wakalat-ul-istimal Agency contract for the use of assets.

Wakeel An agent.

Waqf An Islamic endowment. In Islamic insurance, it is when members' contributions to a trust fund are accumulated by a takaful company, from which members are paid compensation in the future.

Zakah The principle of the purification of wealth and the ruling in Shariah that 2.5% of quantified wealth should be given to the eligible poor.

The manufacturer's authorised representative in the EU is Springer Nature Customer Service Centre GmbH, Europaplatz 3, 69115 Heidelberg, Germany. If you have any concerns regarding our products, please contact ProductSafety@springernature.com

Printed and bound by CPI Group (UK) Ltd, Croydon, CR0 4YY
30/09/2026
02225442-0004